THE LANGUAGE LIBRARY

CHANGING ENGLISH

SIMEON POTTER

Changing English

ANDRE DEUTSCH

FIRST PUBLISHED 1969 BY
ANDRE DEUTSCH LIMITED
105 GREAT RUSSELL STREET
LONDON WC1
COPYRIGHT © 1969 BY SIMEON POTTER
ALL RIGHTS RESERVED
PRINTED IN GREAT BRITAIN BY
TONBRIDGE PRINTERS LTD
TONBRIDGE KENT
233 96059 7

CONTENTS

PREFACE

THIS BOOK is based almost entirely on BBC radio broadcasts given over the last ten years in series of talks on *The English Tongue, Man and his Environment, Language and Languages*, and *English Today*, all four produced by Miss Rosemary Jellis whom I now thank most sincerely for her expert guidance and encouragement. Some of these talks were printed in *The Listener*, and reprinted by permission in various journals in West Africa, India and Japan. Talks and printed texts brought me numerous letters from far and wide, some critical and challenging, others helpful and informative. These letters testified to an astonishingly varied interest in the problems of speech and language. More than ever they made me realize how difficult it may sometimes be to answer the simplest questions on tricky linguistic points fully and satisfactorily. To all these friendly and generous correspondents I take this opportunity of expressing my warmest appreciation and gratitude.

At the request of Dr W. R. Lee, Editor of *English Language Teaching*, I contributed in 1966 two articles on current trends to the May and October issues of that journal. With his kind permission I have drawn upon these articles for many of the illustrations and examples given in Chapters 6 and 7.

Chapter 8 is very largely a revised version of an essay contributed to *Studies in Language and Literature in honour of Margaret Schlauch* published by Państwowe Wydawnictwo Naukowe at Warsaw in that same year.

S.P.

ABBREVIATIONS

AN	Anglo-Norman	Jap.	Japanese
adj.	adjective	Lat.	Latin
adv.	adverb	ME	Middle English
APD	Authors' and Printers' Dictionary	MHG	Middle High German
		O	object
BBC	British Broadcasting Corporation	ODEE	Oxford Dictionary of English Etymology
CG	Common Germanic	OE	Old English
Chin.	Chinese	OED	Oxford English Dictionary
COD	Concise Oxford Dictionary	OF	Old French
Cz.	Czech	OHG	Old High German
E	English	p.	page
EDD	English Dialect Dictionary	P	predicate
		PE	Present-day English
F	French	Pol.	Polish
G	German	Port.	Portuguese
Gk	Greek	pp.	past participle
IE	Indo-European	pron.	pronoun
interj.	interjection	R	indirect object
IPA	International Phonetic Alphabet	RCR	Rules for Compositors and Readers
ITA	Initial Teaching Alphabet	RHD	Random House Dictionary
Ital.	Italian	RP	received pronunciation

Russ.	Russian	SOED	Shorter Oxford English Dictionary
S	subject	v	auxiliary verb
sb.	substantive	V	verb
Skr.	Sanskrit	Webster III	Webster's Third New International Dictionary
Sp.	Spanish		
SPE	Society for Pure English		

SYMBOLS

<	'changed from' or or 'derived from'
>	'changed to' or 'becomes'
[ ]	enclose *phonetic symbols*
/ /	enclose *phonemic symbols*
:	after phonetic symbols denotes *length*
:	between forms denotes *opposition*
/	between forms denotes *alternation*
*	indicates a *reconstructed* or *hypothetical form*

PHONETIC SYMBOLS

The consonant-letters p, b, t, d, k, g; l, r, m, n; f, v, s, z, h, w
have their usual English values. Below are given the key-words
for other sounds appearing in this book:

CONSONANTS

tʃ	*ch*urch	ɲ	F a*gn*eau
dʒ	*j*u*dg*e	ʃ	*sh*ip
ŋ	si*ng*	ʒ	mea*s*ure
θ	*th*in	ç	G i*ch*
ð	*th*en	x	G a*ch*
ʍ	*wh*y	j	*y*es

VOWELS

i:	*see*	ã	F bl*an*c
i	s*i*t	u:	m*oo*n
e	g*e*t	u	p*u*t
a	c*a*t	ʌ	b*u*t
ɑ:	f*a*ther	ə:	b*ir*d
ɔ	h*o*t	ə	fath*er*
ɔ:	f*or*	y	F p*u*r
œ̃	F *un*	φ	F cr*eu*x
ɔ̃	F b*on*	œ	F s*eu*l
ɛ̃	F v*in*	o	F m*o*t

DIPHTHONGS

ei	d*ay*	ɔi	b*oy*
ou	g*o*	iə	h*ere*
ai	fl*y*	ɛə	th*ere*
au	n*ow*	uə	g*our*d

CHAPTER 1

Changing Sounds

OURS WOULD be a dull world if we all spoke alike. It is good that we have our individual ways of speaking and peculiarities of pronunciation. No two of us have exactly the same kinds of lips, teeth, mouth and vocal cords. Predetermined by our physical make-up, our ways of speaking are greatly influenced by our upbringing and education, and they are constantly modified by the society in which we move.

Pronunciation is seldom fixed: it is changing always and everywhere. But there is one powerful factor that restrains pronunciation from changing too quickly at any one time, namely the primary need to be understood. Intelligibility acts like a brake on speech change. The basic function of speech is not individual expression, but intercommunication. You can talk to yourself as you please and make all kinds of extraordinary noises in so doing, but, if you are explaining a thing to somebody else, and if you are not immediately understood, you find this so tedious and exasperating that you make quite sure that you do not have to repeat yourself in future. You are thus bound by necessity to conform to prevailing fashions and to speak normally and understandably.

RECEIVED PRONUNCIATION

Received pronunciation, abbreviated as RP, is the term used by linguists to denote the way of speaking adopted by intelligent and educated people in good conversation. In this book RP records the normal conversation of people living in Greater London and south-east England. It is the pronunciation used by the staff of the British Broadcasting Corporation in their news

13

bulletins, and by many lecturers and entertainers in their radio and television programmes. It is neither better nor worse than West Country speech, or the sonorous language of the Yorkshire dales, or the other surviving dialects of the British Isles, but it happens to be the present form of speech used by careful and responsible speakers in the capital city of the Commonwealth and its surroundings.

Other cities, notably Edinburgh and Dublin, have their received pronunciations, and so have other regions of the English-speaking world: the United States and Canada, South Africa, Australia, and New Zealand. The English language now has unity in diversity. It has more received pronunciations than one.

Notice, by the way, the significance of that epithet *received*. Received by whom? By society in general, and not by professional phoneticians. The term reflects, in fact, an important change of attitude towards language. It may be compared with the notion of *acceptability* which has now superseded that of grammatical correctness. Again, you may say, acceptable to whom? To educated persons in general, to intelligent people who speak and write English efficiently, and not to professional grammarians.

PHONEMIC STRUCTURE

The number of sounds or phones you can articulate is countless. Try, for instance, varying the diphthong in *by* or *buy* [bai] according to all the dialectal and idiolectal pronunciations you have ever heard. You will find that they soon run into dozens. But the time will soon come when you perceive that your diphthong is growing more and more marginal or peripheral, hardly distinguishable from *boy* on the one hand and *bay* on the other. Here, in a somewhat rough and ready (but extremely useful) way, you are confronted with the reality of the *phoneme*. As, by subtle gradations, you glide from [bai] to [bɔi] and from [bai] to [bei], you are actually passing from phoneme to phoneme. Within the system of phonemes, or phonemic structure, of present-day English you overstep the confines of

one contrastive bundle of phones and glide into another bundle
of phones. That is what really constitutes a phoneme. It is a
closely coherent group of sounds contrasting meaningfully with
other groups in the language. At the same time it is the
minimum distinctive unit of sound into which any given flow of
speech can be analysed.

Standard English has 46 phonemes: 12 vowels, 8 diphthongs,
2 semivowels, and 24 consonants. Here they all are, represented
by the agreed symbols of the International Phonetic Alphabet.

Vowels: i: ɑ: ɔ: u: ə:
      i e a ɔ u ʌ ə
Diphthongs: ei ou ai au ɔi
      iə ɛə uə
Semivowels: j w
Consonants: p b t d k g
      tʃ dʒ
      m n ŋ
      f v θ ð s z ʃ ʒ
      l r h

The greatest changes are now taking place in the pronunciation
of diphthongs. Some lesser changes are to be seen in the
pronunciation of long vowels, short vowels, and semivowels,
in that order. Consonant sounds remain fairly stable, but some
are being dropped or inserted in consonant clusters.[1]

CHANGES IN MONOPHTHONGS

Of the five long vowels, as in *see, tar, saw, two* and *sir*, only the
second and the last are now pronounced quite evenly throughout
their duration. You will often hear the high front and high back
vowels /i:/ and /u:/ pronounced with end glides, reminding you
of changes which marked the beginning of the Great Vowel
Shift in the fourteenth century. Thus, instead of *see* [si:], you

---

[1] For fuller accounts of IPA symbols see Daniel Jones, *An Outline of
English Phonetics*, pp. ix-x; A. C. Gimson, *An Introduction to the Pronunciation of English*, pp. 284-5; Simeon Potter, *Modern Linguistics*,
pp. 21–25.

hear [sij], and, instead of *two* [tu:], you hear [tuw]. You hear the lower mid-back /ɔ:/ pronounced with a central vowel or schwa /ə/ as an end glide, or with just a slight centralization towards it. It is not enough, however, to warrant the transcription [sɔə]. Listen carefully, and you will detect a growing tendency to pronounce *saw* and *sore* alike as [sɔ:]. Before the breathed or voiceless fricatives /s, f, θ/ this lower mid-back /ɔ:/ continues to be shortened in *cross, frost, loss, lost, toss; off, office, oft, often, soften; broth* and *cloth*. In the adverb *often* this shortening is frequently accompanied by the restoration of the voiceless dental plosive: [ɔ:fn>ɔfn>ɔftən]. You can hear all three pronunciations, but the last is winning the day. Oddly enough, few people say [sɔftən]. It is, of course, a much less used word. They are therefore unaware of any inconsistency in saying *soft* but *soften* without the *t*, *chaste* but *chasten, fast* but *fasten, haste* but *hasten, list* but *listen, moist* but *moisten*.

Before a velar or dark *l* you hear a diphthongized /ou/ instead of /ɔ/. You hear *solve* [soulv] and *involve* [inˈvoulv] as well as [sɔlv] and [inˈvɔlv]. You hear a distinct /ould/ in *bold, cold, fold, gold, hold, mould, rolled, sold, told* and *wold*. Before -lt, [ɔ] is often lengthened. You hear people say *salt* [sɔ:lt] instead of [sɔlt] and *fault* [fɔ:lt] instead of [fɔlt].

One of the most interesting changes is the gradual lengthening of [a] before final voiced consonants in words like *bad, bag, jam* and *man*. Whereas, for instance, *bad* [bad] and *bard* [bɑ:d] were contrasted by both quality (front versus back) and quantity (short versus long), they now tend to be contrasted by quality alone. Try saying in slow speech 'Scott was not a *bad bard*'. Do you perceive any measurable difference in length between those last two words? Laboratory tests reveal only a slight difference. If this change continues, it may well affect the future phonemic pattern of Standard English.

The contrasts between *bid* and *bead, good* and *food, cod* and *cord*, are still based quite definitely on both quality and quantity, thus distinguishing English from a language like Italian in which all its seven long vowels are just short vowels prolonged. Under American influence the tendency to lengthen short vowels is increasing. The final vowel is often lengthened in

words like *beauty* [bju:ti>bju:ti:] and *city* [siti>siti:],
especially in the plural [bju:ti:z] and [siti:z]. In Edinburgh
Scottish, however, the movement is in the opposite direction.
There all vowels tend to remain short.

In London English you may have observed a regrettable
drift on the part of short vowels towards neutral schwa. You
hear /ʌ/ pronounced /ə/ in words like *cut* [kət] and *cutter*
[kətə], *some* [səm] and *summer* [səmə].

CHANGES IN DIPHTHONGS AND TRIPHTHONGS

By their very nature diphthongs are the least stable sounds in
any language. The five English diphthongs /ei, ou, ai, au, ɔi/
are *closing* and *falling:* closing because, in enunciating them, the
tongue glides from a more open to a closer position in the
mouth; falling because they bear the main stress on the first
element. The first two /ei, ou/ are *narrow:* the tongue moves
through a short space in enunciating them. They are therefore
easily reduced to the simple vowels or monophthongs /e:, o:/.
The remaining three /ai, au, ɔi/ are *wide:* the tongue moves
through a longer space in enunciating them. They are therefore
not easily reduced to monophthongs, but they can be varied in
several ways. Our *house*, for instance, is normally [haus], but
it has many variations [hɑus, həus, heus, hɛus] dialectal and
regional, idiolectal and social. So, too, have its equivalents in
other Germanic languages: German *Haus*, Dutch *huis*, and the
hus(et) of modern Norwegian, Swedish and Danish. The [u:]
of Scandinavian *hus(et)* is, in fact, that long vowel, unchanged
from Common Germanic, which was also preserved in Old and
Middle English, diphthongized in and after the fourteenth
century, and modified in various ways since. Indeed, it would
be no exaggeration to say that we now hear as many variations
in different places as there have been changes in different times
from Chaucer's day to our own.

Increasing numbers of young people pronounce *home* [houm]
as [həum], centralizing the initial element of this narrow
diphthong. This is a prominent and outstanding change because
it is so widespread in all classes of society. There are clear

indications that [həum], not [houm], will be the pronunciation of tomorrow.

A more limited number of people pronounce *late* with a lowered first element [lɛit] or even [lait]. The latter is associated with cockney dialect, but it is by no means limited as a general tendency to that lively and vigorous form of speech. Those speakers who do use the wide diphthong [lait] in *late* are led, unconsciously but ineluctably, to raise and retract the first element of the diphthong in *light* in order to keep these phonemes apart and thus make themselves generally intelligible (p. 13). They therefore say something approaching [lait nɔit], instead of RP [leit nait], for *late night*. On the other hand, young people, aping a more refined level of speech, tend to say [le:t neit]. Between these two extremes, the lowly and the sophisticated, countless varieties of pronunciation can be distinguished.

The three *centring* diphthongs /iə, ɛə, uə/ are so called because, in making them, the tongue glides from a high-front, mid-front or high-back position to one which is central in the mouth and indeed quite neutral. They are peculiar to English since they all arise from the weakening and subsequent loss of the vibrant *r*. This was no longer trilled in the seventeenth century and either weakened to schwa or dropped altogether in the eighteenth. It was weakened to schwa, for instance, in *beard* [biəd] and dropped altogether in *heard* [hə:d]. Today you have perhaps noted a tendency to articulate this /iə/, especially in the final position, as two syllables /i-ə/. You hear *nausea* [nɔ:si-ə], instead of [nɔ:siə], and *magnesia* [mag'ni:zi-ə] for [mag'ni:ʃə] or [mag'ni:ʃiə]. The latter may be regarded as a spelling pronunciation (p. 33). Do you say [jiə] or [jə:] for *year?* Some people say [jiə] *year*, but [jə:li] *yearly*, probably influenced by *early* which everyone pronounces [ə:li]. Clearly [jiə] will be the pronunciation of tomorrow, rhyming with *dear, ear, fear, gear, hear, near, rear*, etc.

The centring diphthong /eə/ is often monophthongized to /ə:/ even by those persons who openly denounce it as a vulgarism or as a most undesirable importation from Merseyside. Instead of [fɛə wɛə ən tɛə] *fair wear and tear* you often hear [fə: wə:r ən tə:], or something approaching it, but it is hardly likely that this unprofitable phonemic merger will ever win general acceptance.

The centring diphthong /uə/ is reasonably stable, but again, as with its front counterpart /iə/ you may have noticed a tendency, especially in final position, to say /u-ə/ as two syllables. You hear [a:dju-əs] and [in'dju-ə] for *arduous* and *endure*.

As we have already seen, the centring diphthong /ɔə/ is still heard, but, because we think it is on its way out (p. 16), we have not given it phonemic status. (If we did, it would raise the number of RP phonemes from 46 to 47.) Normal speakers do not, in reality, make any distinction between *paw* and *pore*, however persistently they assert that they do so. Many Londoners, it should be noted, also say [pɔ:] for *poor*, thus making it homophonous with *paw* and *pore*. Good speakers, however, hold strictly to [puə] rhyming with *boor* and *moor* rather than with *door* and *floor*.

The five triphthongs /eiə, ouə, aiə, auə, ɔiə/ as in *player*, *rower*, *fire*, *hour*, *employer*, are of rare frequency, are of considerable instability, and therefore we have not given them phonemic status. (If we did, we should have to raise the number of RP phonemes from 46 to 51.) These triphthongs all consist of a closing diphthong plus schwa, pronounced as one syllable. Herein, however, lies the dilemma of their instability. If they are articulated with only one breath impulse, they tend to be reduced to diphthongs or even monophthongs. If they are articulated as two syllables, they cease to qualify as genuine triphthongs. Try reciting the couplet in Burns's *Epistle to John Lapraik*—

> *Gie me ae spark o' Nature's fire,*
> *That's a' the learning I desire*

– pronouncing *fire* as a full triphthong [faiə]; as a diphthong plus schwa [fai-ə]; as a diphthong plus schwa with intervening epenthetic semivowel [faijə]; as centring diphthong [faə] or [faə]; and, lastly, as a monophthong [fa:]. To preserve the rhyme your pronunciation of *desire* will, of course, change likewise. Now which of these five pronunciations do you find most impressive? You will certainly hear them all in Greater London. The future of these centring triphthongs, so characteristic of English, is quite uncertain. Who can predict how they will be pronounced in the twenty-first century?

CHANGES IN SEMIVOWELS

After the buccal plosives *p b t d k g,* the glottal *h,* and the nasal plosives *m n,* the palatal semivowel is normally preserved in such type-words as *puny, beauty, tune, due, cue, leguminous, huge, music* and *numeral.* After the lateral *l,* however, and the sibilants *s* and *z,* this *j* is far from stable. Listen to a distinguished senior poet declaiming Milton's prayer to the Holy Spirit –

> *What in me is dark*
> *Illumine, what is low raise and support*

– and you really cannot be sure whether he is saying [i'lju:min] or [i'lu:min], so slight is the palatal glide. Listen to a young undergraduate debater citing Lord Acton's famous dictum 'Power tends to corrupt, and absolute power corrupts absolutely' and you are left in no doubt about transcribing [absəlu:t pauə kə'rʌpts absəlu:tli]. The *j* has gone after *l,* and this is obviously the pronunciation of tomorrow. Young people now say [lu:sid] *lucid* and [lu:t] *lute* or *loot.* They say [lu:nə] *lunar* and [lu:nətik] *lunatic.* They even write *loony.*

After *s* and *z* you still hear both pronunciations: [sju:t] *suit* as well as [su:t], [ə'sju:m] *assume* and [ə'su:m]; [pri'zju:m] *presume* as well as [pri'zu:m], [ri'zju:m] *resume* and [ri'zu:m].

It might be maintained that any shift leading to *neutralization,* or loss of discrimination between contrasting groups of words, involves some detriment to linguistic efficiency. It is a plain loss that some speakers no longer differentiate between *beauty* and *booty; cue* and *coo; cute* and *coot; due, dew* and *do; feud* and *food; mute* and *moot; news* and *noose; tutor* and *tooter.*

By the same token it is a plain loss that some speakers fail to discriminate between *whales* and *Wales; wheel* and *weal; when* and *wen; whether* and *wether; which* and *witch; while* and *wile;*

whine and *wine; whither* and *wither; white* and *wight.* This ancient distinction is indeed well preserved in the northern counties and there are welcome signs that it is becoming fashionable again in the south whether as a normal voiced bilabial preceded by aspiration /hw/ or as a breathed bilabial semivowel /ʍ/.[1]

CONSONANTAL CHANGES

You may have observed an interesting tendency to pronounce words like *warmth, sense* and *length* as [wɔ:mpθ], [sents] and [leŋkθ] instead of historical [wɔ:mθ], [sens] and [leŋθ]. In passing from nasal plosive to breathed fricative you lower your velum a split second too soon and you inadvertently articulate a homorganic buccal plosive. This tendency to insert such *epenthetic* consonant sounds is a quite harmless one. It makes for greater ease in utterance and it is probably increasing.

Another slight but interesting tendency is to be observed in the articulation of the final voiced plosives *b, d* and *g*. These are often partially unvoiced. There is no danger that they will fall in with the voiceless plosives *p, t* and *k* because the latter have strong aspiration. On the contrary, however, intervocalic *t* is often lightly voiced in the American fashion in words like *better, letter* and *matter*. At the moment the glottal plosive is often substituted for *t* in this position, but let us hope that it is only a passing phase.

All varieties of lateral consonants, allophones of the *l* phoneme, are articulated with the tip or blade of the tongue on the alveolus or teethridge. The air stream passes on both sides of the tongue: hence the useful term *lateral*. Before vowels and the semivowel *j* we form a clear *l*, as in *leaf* [li:f] and *million* [miljən]. We form a dark *l* before consonants and finally, as in *field* [fi:ld] and *feel* [fi:l]. Dark *l* is frequently vocalized to *u*

[1] If this sound is fully restored to RP, it will lead to the addition of a consonantal phoneme to the pattern of English, thus raising the number to 47. This is a minor matter, but it is worth observing in this context. The determination of the precise number of phonemes in the synchronic description of a language at any one stage in its history is always arbitrary.

in rapid speech. You hear [oud] for *old*, [auəseuvz]
ourselves, and even [wɛu] for *well*.

In final positions the vibrant *r* is still pronounced when it is
followed in the same breath-group by a word beginning with a
vowel. You naturally say *here* [hiə] but *here and there* [hiər ənd
ðɛə]. This is known as 'linking *r*'. There is indeed nothing
inelegant or inappropriate in its use, and it will certainly be
retained in the speech of tomorrow. It is the English counterpart
of French *liaison*. A Frenchman naturally says *il sent* [il sã] 'he
feels', but *sent-il?* [sãt il] 'does he feel?' He says *faux pas* [fo
pɑ] 'false step, slip, mistake', but *pas un pas* [pɑz œ̃n pɑ] 'not
one step'. An Englishman naturally says *far cry* [fɑ: krai], but
far away [fɑ:r ə'wei]. He says *more light* [mɔ: lait], but *more
and more* [mɔ:r ənd mɔ:].

Today the word-group is undoubtedly increasing in importance at the expense of the word. Many speakers therefore
insert an unetymological or 'intrusive *r*' in such expressions as
the idea of it [ðij ai'diər əv it] on the analogy of *the fear of it*
[ðə fiər av it] where the *r* is, of course, 'linking'. The 'intrusive *r*'
is used even by careful speakers who would be the first, if
challenged, to deny its acceptability. Deny it as they will, they
say *drama and music* [drɑ:mər ənd mju:zik], *area of agreement*
[ɛəriər əv ə'gri:mənt], *Asia and Africa* [ɛiʃər ənd afrikə]. If, in
rapid speech, they deliberately evade this 'intrusive *r*' in such
phrases, they are compelled either to make an artificial juncture
before *and*, or, still worse, to insert a glottal stop; to say either
[eiʃə|| ənd afrikə], or [eiʃəʔ ənd afrikə], thus interrupting
quite unnecessarily the natural flow of discourse.

SIMPLIFICATION OF DOUBLE CONSONANTS

When you say *lamp post*, *boat train* and *black cat*, you do not
normally make two separate *p*, *t* and *k* plosions. You just
lengthen the interval between closing the breath passage and
opening it again. You can, of course, in emphatic speech,
deliberately make two plosions or, in other words, pronounce
two consonants. Contrariwise, you can reduce the double
consonant to a single one and say [lampoust, boutrein, blakat].

There are certainly signs of movement in this direction, but they may denote no more than a passing fashion.

In the noun *partaker* such a simplification did, in fact, win final acceptance. William Tyndale (1526) wrote it as separate words: 'He which throssheth in hope shulde be part taker of his hope' (I Corinthians ix 10). Did he, however, pronounce the two dentals in *part taker* with two distinct plosions or as a double consonant? The authors of the King James Bible (1611) left no one in doubt when they wrote: 'He that thresheth in hope should be partaker of his hope'. Later the verb *partake* was back-formed from the agent noun (p. 83).

SHIFTING STRESS

Ours is a strongly stressed language, resembling Russian more closely than any other great language in this respect. But main stresses in polysyllabic words are more prone to shift in English than they are in Russian. Take, for instance, the word *laboratory*. At the turn of the century '*laboratory* was the accepted pronunciation, especially at Cambridge. Undergraduates said *lab*, and this clipped form (p. 77) is still current even in formal contexts. Today the pronunciation [lə'bɔrətri] is universal. Because the vowel of the penultimate syllable is dropped, this somewhat cumbersome word is brought into line with scores of other polysyllabic words of Greek and Latin provenance that show dactylic rhythms and bear stress on antepenultimate syllables: *aphrodisiac, euthanasia, hippopotamus, hydrophobia, kleptomania, metamorphosis, neurasthenia, schizophrenia* from Greek; *antiquarian, constitutional, magnanimity, notoriety, opportunity, personality, pertinacity, possibility* from Latin. Whatever their morphological structures, the stress patterns of these words are identical: 2 4 1 5 3 where 1 denotes the main stress and 5 the weakest stress. (Test this generalization for yourself. Pronounce each word with distinct division of syllables and feel the satisfying alternation of stronger and weaker stresses.)

Observe the shifting stresses in the following triads of related forms:

ˈdemon	deˈmoniac	demoˈniacal
ˈfamily	faˈmiliar	familiˈarity
ˈhistory	hiˈstorical	histoˈricity
ˈmetropole	meˈtropolis	metroˈpolitan
ˈperiod	periˈodical	perioˈdicity
ˈphotograph	phoˈtography	photoˈgraphical
ˈpyramid	pyˈramidal	pyraˈmidion
ˈtelephone	teˈlephony	teleˈphonic(al)

In words of four syllables there remain some unresolved clashes between the principles of dactylic rhythm and recessive stress. Do you say ˈcontroversy or conˈtroversy? Cassius (in Shakespeare's *Julius Caesar* I ii 107) clearly preferred the former:

> *The torrent roared, and we did buffet it*
> *With lusty sinews, throwing it aside*
> *And stemming it with hearts of controversy.*

But *conˈtroversy*, long general in the north, is now gaining ground in the south. So also, since 1960, *kiˈlometer* has superseded ˈ*kilometer*, and, with the adoption of the decimal system in the world of sport, it will certainly hold its own. Otherwise, in many tetrasyllabic words the conflict between initial and antepenultimate stress remains unsettled – in such forms as *applicable, commendable, comparable, contumacy, despicable, formidable, hospitable, illustrative, intricacy, lamentable, migratory, pejorative* and *reputable*. Initial stress, however, here bears the cachet of elegance and it will probably prevail.

SHORTENED ANTEPENULTS

You instinctively say *nation* [neiʃən] but *national* [naʃənəl], shortening the diphthong to a monophthong in order to make the adjectival derivative isochronous with its nominal base. You say *choral: chŏrister, code: cŏdify, cycle: cўclamen* and *encўclical, drama: drămatist, dynast: dỹnasty, equal: ĕquable, ĕquinox* and *ĕquity, fable: făbulous, globe: glŏbular, grave: grăvity, holy: hŏliday, inane: inănity, obscene: obscĕnity, omen: ŏminous, onus: ŏnerous, patron: pătronage, private: prĭvacy, profane: profănity, stable: stăbilize, supreme: suprĕmacy, table: tăbular* and *tăbulate,* and so on. This is an ancient and honourable prosodic principle in our language and it is painful, if not excruciating, to hear people vacillating between [ɔnərəs] and [ounərəs] or between [dramətist] and [drɑːmətist]. Alas, even educated people sometimes lack *Sprachgefühl,* that innate feeling for the harmony of language.

There are many exceptions to this simple rule – inevitable in a language of such multifarious origins. *Amenity,* one might argue, falls outside it because this abstract noun is more likely to be a direct adaptation of Latin *amoenitas* than a borrowing of French *aménité;* and the adjective *amene,* though frequently used in Scotland, is seldom heard south of the border. In its plural form *amenities* it is a vogue word (p. 46) much in favour with estate agents and advertisers of holiday resorts. It is to their credit that the pronunciation [əˈmenitiz] seems to be winning the day. And what about *piracy?* Far from being dead, this illicit activity is ever assuming new shapes in this technological age and its old nineteenth-century pronunciation [pirəsi] is certainly on its way back.

MORE STANDARDS THAN ONE

As we look beyond the shores of Britain to the rest of the English-speaking world we realize that in this matter of received pronunciation there are more standards than one. In his editorial preface to *Webster's Third New International Dictionary Unabridged* of 1961 (henceforth called Webster III) Dr Philip Babcock Gove makes the point that the pronunciations he records are those 'prevailing in general cultivated conversational usage, both informal and formal, throughout the English-speaking world' and that they can be 'checked today by television, radio and recordings'. In fact, all the first pronunciations in Webster III are, as indeed we should expect, North American.

In the coming centuries the cultivated conversational usages of the great cities – London, Edinburgh, Dublin, Boston, New York, Chicago, Toronto, Cape Town, Sydney and Wellington

– will compete healthily and advantageously, and they will influence one another inevitably and continuously. Most sensible people would now agree that the restoration of fuller qualities to the vowels of weakly stressed syllables in London English is entirely due to North American influence and that it makes for greater clarity and distinctness. That influence is surprisingly recent. It became apparent only in the fourth and fifth decades of this century. Even in old age Robert Bridges (1844–1930) continued to deplore the 'derderderderdiness' of RP, by which, of course, he meant the preponderance of schwa sounds and the appalling monotony of successive stressless syllables. The gradual levelling up and strengthening of weakly stressed vowels in words like *temporary* and *primarily* is surely winning its way into British English.

NORTH AMERICA

It is well known that the speech of North America has preserved features of pronunciation and lexis that have been lost in European English. The same is true of the French of Quebec in its relation to European French. In some particulars, to be sure, it is closer to Voltaire than is the speech of modern Paris.

Canadian pronunciation differs little from that of the contiguous states of its southern neighbour. Its most populous regions lie in the St Lawrence basin and in the lands bordering on Lakes Erie and Ontario. This means that most Canadians live within one hundred miles of the open United States frontier. The influence of United States English is therefore powerful and incessant. In his *Linguistic Atlas of the United States and Canada* Hans Kurath recognizes no isogloss coincident with the political border along Latitude 49°N. The significant linguistic boundary lies well south of the Great Lakes, passing through Ohio, Indiana, Illinois and Iowa.

The speech of the whole of North America has been affected in varying degrees by the influx of European and Asian immigrants during the last one and a half centuries. Ninety per cent of the people who settled on the Atlantic Seaboard before the confirmation of the Federal Constitution in 1787 came from

Britain, but in the ensuing century many millions came from other European countries. Many Germans settled in Pennsylvania, Oregon and the Middle West. After the Civil War many Scandinavians, Slavs and Italians crossed the Atlantic Ocean. This flow of European immigrants was prolonged and it increased in the second quarter of the twentieth century when untold millions fled from Nazi tyranny. Meantime, Spanish-speaking Mexicans and Puerto Ricans continued to pour in from the south.

The cumulative influence of these foreign elements has become especially apparent in the general smoothing and downtoning of dynamic stress. The murmur-vowel schwa is employed to varying extents in German, French and Russian. It is not heard at all in Spanish, Italian and Czech, and these three languages are all spoken with clear and distinct demarcation of syllables. Consequently American speech has become, like Spanish and Italian, predominantly *staccato* and *marcato*, whereas British English remains, like Polish and Russian, *legato* and *glissando*. In some ways American speech is more monotonous than British, but its meanings are far more easily assimilable. It makes fewer demands upon the hearer's attention and it is less assertive, less aggressive. Many Americans speak with small variety of tone. Their tempo is slower. Many speakers of the American Midland dialect allow soft palate and velum to droop, imbuing their speech with a nasal twang which assumes diverse variations from state to state and from person to person.

Dialectal differences are more marked in England between Trent and Tweed than in the whole of North America. For three centuries and more American families have been continually on the move. Speech communities have seldom lived in isolation for more than one generation. The Northern Dialect embraces part of the northern states and the whole of Canada. The Midland or General Dialect includes New York City and State west of the Hudson River, as well as all the Midland and Western states, thus covering two thirds of the population and four fifths of the land surface of the Federal Republic from coast to coast. The New England Dialect is

spoken in Maine, New Hampshire, Vermont, Massachusetts,
Rhode Island, Connecticut, and that strip of New York State
which lies east of the Hudson River. This dialect is closest to
British RP and many of its speakers endeavour to make themselves as English as possible. They preserve the rounded vowel
in *dock* [dɔk] as against the low back vowel in Midland [dɑk],
this same low back vowel in dance [dɑ:ns] as against the front
vowel in Midland [da:ns], and the compensatorily lengthened
vowel in *dark* [dɑ:k] as against the shorter front vowel with
vibrant retained in Midland [dark]. Boston stands within the
borders of this New England Dialect, and so do the Universities
of Harvard and Yale, and the Massachusetts Institute of
Technology, which have close ties with Western Europe in the
world of learning. The Southern Dialect includes Maryland,
Virginia, North and South Carolina, Georgia, Florida, Kentucky, Tennessee, Alabama, Mississippi, Arkansas and Louisi-
ana, together with a large area of Missouri, Oklahoma and
Texas. With the exception of Delaware and West Virginia, it is
spoken in all the states lying south of Pennsylvania and the
Ohio River and east of a line running from St Louis to the
Colorado and then down that river to the Gulf of Mexico.

The influence of American pronunciation on British, Australian and other regional varieties of English will increase in
future and will lead inevitably to a certain levelling out of
divergences and inequalities. Even today dialectal differences
are smaller throughout the widely diffused English-speaking
world than they were within the narrow confines of fourteenth-
century England.

AFRICA

In South Africa the pronunciation of English remains fairly
stable although it has to co-exist daily with Afrikaans, a
simplified form of European Dutch. English-speaking South
Africans have left the Commonwealth politically, but they look
to Britain culturally. They are acutely conscious that they stand
on the defensive linguistically. They therefore discourage the
development of any distinctively South African dialect. On the

whole they follow London pronunciation. For instance, they give more open sounds to the first elements of the diphthongs in *day* and *gate*.

In the West African Territories – Gambia, Sierra Leone, Ghana and Nigeria – speakers of English favour a careful and academic pronunciation. These four states achieved autonomy in that one decade, 1955 to 1965, which saw the withdrawal of all European rule (except Portuguese) from Africa. Two native languages, Hausa and Swahili, compete with English as media of interstate trade and communication. Nascent universities still rely upon the University of London, which sponsored them, for direction and guidance.

INDIA AND PAKISTAN

Many millions of Indians and Pakistanis carry over into their pronunciation of English the prosodic features of Hindi and Urdu, rattling off sequences of syllables at top speed with all the repetitive monotony of machine gun fire. They interlard their discourse with spelling pronunciations unheard beyond the confines of the subcontinent. Too often their enunciation is lax and imprecise.

They admit that theirs is clerk's language', called disparagingly Babu English, a term relating, however, more to lexis and syntax than to pronunciation. Those who are content to express themselves in Babu English have little regard for those significant choices of word and phrase which differentiate registers of speech, whether archaic, literary, common, colloquial or slang.

What of the future? It is quite uncertain. In 1950 the Constitution of the Republic ruled that Hindi should be the official language of India, but that English should remain in use for a further fifteen years. In 1965, however, when this moratorium ended, the necessity of English for interstate communication was seen by responsible authorities to be greater than ever. In a public proclamation in 1967 the Prime Minister prescribed that English should be retained indefinitely as the one international language of India. Renewed efforts were then

made to improve the teaching of English in schools and
universities, however unpromising the preconditions for such
improvements might be in a country where qualified instructors
were scarce and where the masses remained stubbornly illiterate.

AUSTRALIA

Australian English has slower rhythms and flatter intonations
than British RP. The neutral schwa is far too much in evidence,
giving a cockney colouring to daily talk, especially to the speech
of the only two large cities, Sydney and Melbourne. *Archers* and
arches both become [ɑːtʃəz]. Conversely, Australians distinguish between *taxis* [ˈtaksiz] and *taxes* [ˈtaksəz] and between
candied [ˈkandid] and *candid* [ˈkandəd] which in RP are homophonous. The lengthening of the final vowel in *beauty* [bjuːtiː]
and *city* [ˈsitiː], which we have already seen to be a growing
feature of RP itself (p. 17), is widespread. Moreover, *receive*
sounds like [riːsiːv], its two syllables acquiring equal duration
and level stress.

Without going into details we may observe that the long
vowels /iː/ and /uː/ and the diphthongs /ei/ and /ai/ have
shifted their positions within the Australian phonemic pattern
under American influence. Various degrees of nasalization can
also be detected, probably, but by no means demonstrably,
under American impact. It is indeed inevitable that Australia
should depend more and more upon the United States both
politically and culturally. The influence of American English
upon the whole of Australia and Tasmania will surely increase
in the coming years.

NEW ZEALAND

New Zealand remains 'the most British of all the Dominions'.
It has, for instance, offered steadfast and successful resistance
to Yankee nasalization. Antipodean universities draw heavily
upon the six ancient universities of England and Scotland in
their recruitment of young teachers. Otherwise, of course, New
Zealand English resembles the Australian variety in the main,

at the same time showing noteworthy divergences between North and South Islands. It differs from Australian in retaining the long back vowel sound in *chance, dance, lance* and *slant*, and in refusing to develop a schwa-coloured on-glide in *do, true, two* and *you*. On the other hand, it exhibits a high front palatal glide in *yes* [jiəs] and *yet* [jiət], by which alone, it is said, New Zealanders are infallibly recognized abroad. *Throne* [θroun] and *thrown* [θrouən] are not homophones as in RP, nor are *groan* and *grown* or *moan* and *mown*. The intervocalic sibilants are voiced in Asia [eiʒə] and Persia [pə:ʒə].

Whereas the aborigines have exerted no discernible influence on Australian speech, the Maoris of New Zealand, who are more numerous in North Island, have contributed something good to current speech in so far as they have helped to preserve its sonority and to retard that ubiquitous drift towards neutral schwa. The Maoris migrated from south-east Asia as long ago as the fourteenth century. Their own language belongs to the Malayo-Polynesian family and it is akin to Tahitian, Samoan and Hawaian. When educated Maoris speak English, they do so with precision and grace. Meantime the Maori language itself survives. It competes with Classical Latin in providing schools and public buildings with lapidary inscriptions.

FOREIGN PLACE-NAMES

Earlier in this century everyone spoke of the River Seine, Cherbourg, Majorca, Sofia and Buenos Aires as the [sein, ʃə:bə:g, mə'dʒɔ:kə, sə'faiə and [bju:enouz ɛəz], but many now say [sen, ʃɛr'bu:r, ma'jɔrka, soufiə] and [bwenos airis], often with delightful and commendable precision. Elderly cynics, it is true, shake their heads, scorning these new sounds as affected and pedantic. Besides, is it really *de bon ton* to display one's superior knowledge of foreign tongues and to swagger about the extent of one's travels abroad?

The pronunciation of names in the modern world is surely too vital and important to warrant the adoption of such frivolous attitudes. Wake up, England! Any movement away from parochialism and insularity is in these days beneficial and salutary. Ideally, every place-name should be enunciated exactly as its inhabitants pronounce it when they speak formally and officially.

At once, however, many difficulties arise. Venezia [veˈne: tsia], Pearl of the Adriatic, is immortalized in Shakespeare's *The Merchant of Venice* and Ruskin's *The Stones of Venice.* The French call it *Venise,* the Germans *Venedig,* and the Czechs *Benátky.* Firenze [fiˈrentse], city of Dante and Michelangelo and the Medici, is likewise immortalized in Browning's *Old Pictures in Florence.* It was *Florentia* to the Romans of two thousand years ago. Bratislava on the Danube is so named by Czechs and Slovaks, but its German-speaking natives still call it *Pressburg* and its Hungarian inhabitants call it *Pozorny.* All three names are genuine and historical.

The Universal Postal Union, now UPU, a constituent organization of the United Nations, was established at Berne in 1874. It has recently made a world survey of place-names in authenticated romanized script to which Russia, China and the thirteen Arab states have gladly contributed.

FOREIGN WORDS AND PHRASES

Young people who travel abroad and who hear foreign expressions rightly pronounced on radio and television programmes are not likely to put up with old-fashioned approximations that passed muster even in educated circles some years ago. Students of all ages now have their language laboratories and many other forms of audio-visual aids. Their general approach to the language-learning business has lost something in depth, but it has gained considerably in width. Their whole attitude towards the practical study of languages ancient and modern is now far more flexible and adaptable than it was in the first half of the twentieth century.

On Sunday, 25 June 1967, the first global telecast was achieved. This linkup was made possible only by the employment of earth satellites, microwaves and landlines. Behind translated speeches the voices of participants could be clearly heard in the original tongues, thus enabling viewers to enjoy

well-spoken conversation in defined situational contexts. More
and more foreign films will be shown on television screens
accompanied by native sound tracks, but supplemented by
English captions, so that linguists will have incomparable
opportunities of keeping up their knowledge of living tongues
and of combining instruction with entertainment.

SPELLING PRONUNCIATION

When all is said and done, it must be at last admitted that the
most numerous, insidious and continuous changes in the
pronunciation of PE arise from the influence of the written and
printed spellings of words upon their spoken sounds. A changed
spoken form arising from such influence is known technically as
a *spelling pronunciation*, German *Schreibungaussprache*.

Where literacy is advanced, the eye takes precedence of the
ear. In an industrial society people like to be fashionable and up
to date and they like to be understood easily and promptly, but
they are very little concerned with etymology and linguistic
history. They have far larger passive than active vocabularies.
They apprehend at once the meanings of many hundreds of
words when they read or hear them, but they themselves never
think of using these words in their own speech or writing.
(You can easily verify this for yourself. Think now of half a
dozen expressions which you fully understand but which you
never have occasion to use in your daily affairs.)

Spelling pronunciations have greatly increased since the
passing of the Ewart Public Libraries Act of 1850 and the
Forster Education Act of 1870, but they were operative long
before the nineteenth century. They began as soon as ever the
gap between written and spoken forms became sufficiently
marked. The professional clerks of the Middle Ages had their
scribal traditions, but on the whole (to their great credit) they
wrote phonetically. When, in the fifteenth century, many men
and women (like the members of the Paston family in Norfolk)
who were not trained clerks began to write, they spelt pretty
well as they chose. Provided that they were understood, they
had neither time nor need to worry about niceties. Our spelling

B

today is largely that of the fourteenth and fifteenth centuries – the late ME period. Since then it has remained fairly static, but pronunciation has been constantly changing and it will never cease to change in future.

Many spelling pronunciations are slight, almost imperceptible, and quite harmless, but their cumulative results may be considerable. Take, for instance, all words ending in -*ture*. Do you say [tʃə] or [tjə] or [tjuə]? Do you say [neitʃə] or [neitjə] or [neitjuə] for *nature?* The Romans said *nātūra* (Lat. *nāscī, nātus* 'to be born', older *gnāscī, gnātus*, formed from the root **gn* or **gen*). Chaucer said [naːtyːr], OF having fronted that second Latin vowel and dropped the inflexion. Later his readers said [naːtiur], substituting /iu/ for OF and AN /yː/, and, later still, they tended to make the first element a consonant and said [naːtjur]. Now it so happens that the shift from /tj/ to the affricate /tʃ/ is easy – so easy as to be almost inevitable. (Children say [tʃuːn] for RP [tjuːn] *tune* and [tʃuːlip] for RP [tjuːlip] *tulip*.) Shakespeare said [nɛːtʃuər] and Pope [neːtʃuə] or [neːtʃə]. In RP, where /eː/ has been diphthongized to /ei/, the pronunciation is [neitʃə]. If, then, you persist in saying [neitjə] or [neitjuə] you are deliberately preferring a more difficult pronunciation than the accepted one and it is consciousness of the spelling alone that makes you do so.

Again, do you pronounce the middle *t* in *chestnut?* In rapid speech you certainly do not because consonant clusters like -*stn*- (*chestnut, fastening*) and -*stm*- (*Christmas, postman*) are by no means easy to articulate. The first component of *chestnut* has its origin in a place-name – probably Castana in Thessaly. This lovely Mediterranean tree was known to the Anglo-Saxons and they called it *cisten bēam* and its fruit *cisten hnutu*. This latter became ME *chesten nut*, but the breathed dental plosive of *chesten* was dropped early. 'Your chessenut was ever the only colour' said Celia to Rosalind (in *As You Like It*, III iv 13) pronouncing *chessenut* still as a word of three syllables and referring to that favourite hue, deep reddish-brown. For some centuries *chesnut* was the accepted orthography. That majestic one-mile grove in Bushy Park leading south from Teddington to the Lion Gate, Hampton Court, was named

Chesnut Avenue by King William III who planted it. *Chesnut* was indeed the only form in Nathaniel Bailey's Dictionary of 1721 and in all its later editions. It was Samuel Johnson who restored the *t* in his Dictionary of 1755 and he has been followed by all subsequent lexicographers. When you hear careful speakers going out of their way to say [tʃest||n ʌ t], making an unnatural pause after a precisely articulated dental, it is amusing to reflect that they do so by the arbitrament of the great Doctor alone, who, temperamentally conservative, claimed 'not to disturb, upon narrower views, or for minute propriety, the orthography of his fathers'.

In Webster III of 1961 [klə:k] is given as the accepted pronunciation of *clerk* in the United States, but the British [klɑ:k] had been duly recorded as a dialectal pronunciation in the state of Kentucky in Webster II of 1934. No one in Britain or America now says [klɑ:dʒi], but this was the pronunciation (and *clargy* was the spelling, side by side with *clergy*) for three centuries at least. Berkhampstead [bɑ:kəmstid] has changed both spelling and pronunciation within living memory. It is now officially spelt *Berkhamsted* and pronounced [bə:kəmsted]. Hundreds of English towns and villages are now known by two names, the local and the non-local, the ancestral and the sophisticated, the old and the new: Cholmondeley, Cirencester, Daventry, Greenwich, Happisburgh, (High) Roding, Leominster, Snettisham, Southwell, Stanwell, Towcester and Wrotham, to cite just a very few at random. Exceptionally interesting are names in–*ham* preceded by an element ending in *s* or *t* which inevitably becomes merged with the following *h* to give spelling pronunciations in *sh* and *th*. Lewisham, for example, OE *Lēofsiges hām* 'Leofsige's homestead', was [ljuisəm] at the turn of the century. Now a Greater London Borough, everyone calls it [ljuiʃəm] or [luiʃəm]. So *Heysham*, OE *hǣs hām* 'homestead in brushwood', is now pronounced [hi:ʃəm]; *Newsham*, OE *(æt þǣm) nēowum hūsum* 'at the new houses', is [nju:ʃəm]; even as *Feltham*, OE *feld hām* 'homestead in open country', becomes [felθəm], and *Waltham*, OE *wald hām* 'forest homestead', becomes [wɔ:lðəm].

To linguistically hypersensitive persons spelling pronunciations are often irritating, even agonizing – Asian [eisiən], controversial [kɔntrə'vəːsiəl], species [spiːsiz], thymol [θaimɔl] – but they are everywhere gaining ground. Their only merit is that they help to narrow that gap between sound and symbol which was probably widest in the Augustan Age when the operation of the Great Vowel Shift was nearing its close, and when 'late, very late, correctness grew our care'.

CHAPTER 2

Reformed Spelling

IT IS well known that English has the most unphonetic spelling among the great languages of the world, with French as a close second. But whereas French spelling is systematically unphonetic, English is unsystematically unphonetic. In the Picard dialect of French the word for 'water' is pronounced [jau] with the initial vowel of *eau* consonantized: Lat. *aqua*, Ital. *acqua*, Sp. *agua*. In Parisian French the word for 'water' is pronounced [o], but so are other words in *eau* like *beau* [bo] 'beautiful', *château* [ʃato] 'castle', *bureau* [byro] 'desk', *sceau* [so] 'seal, stamp', and *vaisseau* [vɛso] 'ship'.

What, then, is to be the future of our unsystematic spelling? Are we to go on suffering it indefinitely? From time to time spelling reform is discussed in the press or on radio and television as if it were something new and as if our inadequate orthography persisted from sheer inertia. In fact, however, every century has had its advocates of reform ever since the thirteenth when an Augustinian Canon named Orm or Ormin devised his own method of distinguishing short vowels from long by doubling the succeeding consonants or, when this was not feasible, by marking short vowels with a superimposed breve. William Caxton, who set up his wooden printing press at the sign of the Red Pale in the Almonry at Westminster in 1476, was fully aware of that widening gap between sound and symbol that we were discussing in Chapter One and he deliberately adopted certain spellings (not always advisedly) in the interests of consistency and uniformity. In 1568, when Shakespeare was a boy of four, Sir Thomas Smith, Secretary of State to Queen Elizabeth, published an imaginary Latin dialogue between himself and a youth Quintus, in which he went so far as to propose a new alphabet of thirty-four letters. In the ensuing year John Hart, 'Chester Herald', used diacritical marks to distinguish vowel sounds and he devised new symbols for consonants. He was not so drastic as his contemporary William Bullokar, a schoolmaster and grammarian, who, in his *Booke at Large*, employed numerous marks, both beneath letters and above, to assist his readers. Little did he know what dangerous proposals he was making! Had the printers followed him in these momentous years, English might have been afflicted by those unfortunate accent-marks and diacritics that in varying degrees hamper the easy writing of French, German, Italian, Spanish, Czech, Polish, Norwegian, Danish, Swedish, and even (outside Indo-European) Finnish and Turkish. Fortunately, no one took Bullokar seriously.[1] He was soon outshone by Richard Mulcaster, a sensible and practical schoolmaster and a man of liberal and independent mind, who saw further ahead than Smith, Hart and Bullokar; further ahead, indeed, than many spelling reformers of his own and subsequent generations.

THE CASE AGAINST DRASTIC REFORM

Richard Mulcaster enjoyed length of days (1530–1611), living under five sovereigns from Henry VIII to James I. While he was Headmaster of Merchant Taylors' School he numbered Edmund Spenser and Lancelot Andrewes among his pupils. When the latter was Bishop of Winchester and member of that

[1] The apostrophe (now much diminished in use), the diaeresis (now obsolescent) and the supraliteral dot (over *i* and *j*) are, most fortunately, our only diacritics. The latter is a nuisance. How many writers place their dots precisely where they should be placed? In writing Greek you dot no iotas. No Latin manuscripts have supraliteral dots before the twelfth century when, for the first time, they were used to distinguish i more clearly since it was liable, especially in cursive script, to be taken as one of the strokes of an adjacent letter. An undotted *j* had begun as a mere final tailed *i* in Classical Latin in numerals like vij and in words like filij 'of the son'. The letters i and j were first taken as two separate symbols in fifteenth-century Spanish. They did not become separate letters in English until the seventeeth century.

committee of divines which produced the King James Bible, he was happy to have his headmaster's portrait hanging over his study door. Later Mulcaster became High Master of St Paul's, and he ended his days as Rector of Stanford Rivers in Essex. He found time to write two books which he called *Positions* (1581) and *The First Part of the Elementary, Which Entreateth Chiefly of the Right Writing of our English Tongue* (1582). By *Positions* he meant *proposals* (for educational reform). *The First Part of the Elementary* was not, in the event, followed by any subsequent part. It was itself an adequate expression of its author's advanced views on teaching, and its *Peroration* contained that passionate outburst of genuine patriotism which linked life closely with language: 'I love Rome, but London better; I favor Italy, but England more; I honor the Latin, but I worship the English'.[1]

Mulcaster saw clearly that there were two insuperable obstacles to drastic reform. First, pronunciation is not uniform over those areas where the language is spoken. Secondly, pronunciation is not static, but is ever changing. Today a drastic reform will satisfy only one section of the community. Tomorrow a drastic reform will satisfy no one. These obstacles remain, *mutatis mutandis*, now in the twentieth century.[2]

Mulcaster therefore recommended no change in the existing twenty-four letters, or *characts*, as he called them (twenty-four, and not twenty-six as now, because *j* and *v* were still included under *i* and *u*). This recommendation carried weight because Mulcaster's influence was considerable. Ben Jonson read his books and quoted from them; sometimes, indeed, without

---

[1] Notice the spelling of *favor* and *honor* (see page 41) and the use of the definite article in *the Latin* and *the English* (page 144). 'I favor' means 'I like, I have kindly feelings towards'. These famous words were echoed (maybe subconsciously) by Sir Winston Churchill in *My Early Life*: '(We are) all biassed in favour of children learning English; and then we would let the clever ones learn Latin as an honour, and Greek as a treat.'

[2] A third obstacle to drastic spelling reform was implicit in Mulcaster's *Elementary*, namely the existence of printed texts. The millions of volumes in the public and private libraries of the world would become 'closed books' (without special study) to the children of tomorrow.

acknowledgement. But Mulcaster's influence was not wide enough to achieve consistency in Tudor spelling. He drew up a General Table of some seven thousand commonest words, but spelling continued to be irregular. For one thing, printers deliberately varied the forms of words in order to *justify* their lines of type and produce straight margins. The typographical flexibility of modern printing, by which letters can be opened out or crowded together at need, was then unknown. When Tudor compositors found themselves pressed for space, they printed *ye* and *yt* for *the* and *that*. When, on the other hand, they wanted to fill out a line, they printed *only* with five letters as *onely, onlie* or *onlye;* with six letters as *onelie* or *onelye;* with seven letters as *onelich* or *onelych;* with eight letters as *oneliche* or *onelyche;* and even with nine letters (including an epenthetic *d*) as *ondeliche* or *ondelyche*. They printed *holines, holiness, holinesse; hoolines, hooliness* or *hoolinesse,* according to space requirements.[1]

STABILIZATION OF ORTHOGRAPHY

Mulcaster lived long enough to see the appearance of the first all-English dictionary – Robert Cawdrey's *A Table Alphabeticall* (1604) – and, in the last year of his life, the completion of the King James Bible (1611), whose wide dissemination among devout readers contributed greatly towards the fixing of English spelling. That process of stabilization was further hastened by the Civil War (1642–46). As Sir William Craigie has clearly shown,[2] compositors had to print political pamphlets in great haste and they had no time 'to think of more than one way of spelling a word, even for the sake of producing a better-spaced line'. That process was further strengthened by the proponents of correctness in the Augustan Age and by that famous lexicographer whose *Dictionary of the English Language* was

---

[1] Since OE *hālignes* belonged to the class of feminine- *jō* stems, and since, as an abstract noun, it was not used in the plural, it had only two well-defined forms in Early West Saxon: *hālignes* in the nominative, and *hālignesse* in its oblique cases.

[2] *Some Anomalies of Spelling,* S.P.E. Tract No. LIX (1942), p. 307.

published in 1755. Unfortunately, in spite of his expressed intention to remove irregularities, Johnson himself was not always consistent. Inadvertently he wrote *amorous* but *amourously, moveable* but *immovable, downhil* but *uphill, distil* but *instill, install* but *reinstal, sliness* but *slyly, conceit* and *deceit* but *receipt, deign* but *disdain, anteriour* and *interiour* but *exterior* and *posterior*.

In assessing the influence of Johnson's Dictionary on the stabilization of our orthography, two facts should be borne in mind: a one-volume *Abridgement* appeared in 1756, and two extensive revisions were made in 1818 and 1866. The *Abridgement* brought guidance to many people who had no access to the larger work.[1] The revisions prolonged the usefulness of Johnson's work into later generations, long after the appearance of Webster in the New World and of the Oxford Dictionary in the Old.

The first revision of Johnson by Archdeacon Henry John Todd was used by Noah Webster whose *American Dictionary of the English Language* appeared in 1828. As a teacher in the backwoods, Webster had found his work made difficult by the vagaries of the traditional orthography. A born nonconformist, he favoured sweeping changes, but he was soon restrained by ineluctable realities. 'Common sense,' he averred, 'would lead me to write *public, favor, nabor, hed, proov, flem, hiz, giv, det, ruf,* and *wel* instead of *publick, favour, neighbour, head, prove, phlegm, his, give, debt, rough* and *well.*' But he soon realized that his Dictionary would have few purchasers if he persisted in such changes. However little he liked the British, he very much wanted them to buy his books. Only the first two new spellings, therefore, were permitted to remain. The spelling *public* has since been adopted, gradually and tacitly, into British English, as also for all other adjectives and nouns in *-ic* from F *-ique*, Lat.*-icus*, or Gk *-ikos*. Unfortunately the spelling *favor* has not yet been accepted. Agent nouns, it is true, have all gone over

---

[1] This was the *Dixonary* that that Johnsonian devotee, Miss Pinkerton, presented as a parting gift to pupils leaving her Academy on Chiswick Mall (Thackeray's *Vanity Fair*, Chapter I). Becky Sharp, you will recall, threw her copy into the garden as the coach drove off.

to -*or* with the exception of *paviour* and *Saviour*. *Governor* was
the last to go over, shedding its redundant -*u*- as late as the
nineteenth century. Non-agent nouns, however, like *ardour*,
behaviour, *clamour*, *colour*, *endeavour*, *honour*, *humour*, *odour*,
rigour, *rumour*, *succour*, *valour* and *vigour* keep the old spelling
side by side with a few in -*or* like *horror*, *pallor*, *terror* and *tremor*.
Derivative adjectives in -*ous* are formed from -*or* (*humorous*),
those in -*able* from -*our* (*honourable*), whereas nouns in -*ist* have
long remained in uncertain transition. Thackeray lectured on
The English Humourists of the Eighteenth Century in 1851, but
long before that, in *The Spectator* No. 477, Addison had told
his readers that he was 'looked upon as an Humorist in
Gardening'. Galsworthy should certainly have known better
(as Eric Partridge reminds us in *Usage and Abusage*, p. 226)
than to have written 'The rumourous town still hummed' in
The Silver Spoon. Clearly we should have done well to follow
old Noah in adhering to -*or* spellings for agent and non-agent
nouns alike, and in accepting -*ize* as the only suffix for all verbs
deriving directly or indirectly from Gk -*izein* and Lat. -*izare*.

UNO is, in fact, the United Nations Organization, not
Organisation. The reason for allowing the latter as an alternative spelling is truly astounding. Concessions, it is argued,
must be made to uneducated people who 'cannot be bothered'
to distinguish between the formations of verbs like *real-ize* and
sur-prise. Because such people are not interested in etymology
and because verbs like *surprise* are so spelt, why should they not
write -*ise* for all verbs ending in [aiz] irrespective of meaning
and history? Whereas, however, there are only some two
dozen common verbs in -*ise* – *advertise*, *advise*, *apprise*, *chastise*,
circumcise, *comprise*, *compromise*, *demise*, *despise*, *devise*, *dis-
franchise*, *disguise*, *enfranchise*, *enterprise*, *excise*, *exercise*, *franchise*, *improvise*, *incise*, *premise*, *revise*, *supervise*, *surmise*, *surprise*
and *televise* – the number of verbs in -*ize* is countless because it
is a living suffix. It is also a very useful suffix because it allows
us to say in one word what would otherwise require a phrase:
to *alphabetize* (a list of names), *anglicize* (a foreign expression),
cannibalize (disused machines), *comprehensivize* (a school
system), *decasualize* (dock labour), *decentralize* (business

administration), *demilitarize* (a frontier zone), *departmentalize* (an institution that has grown unwieldy), *deratize* (a rat-infested building site), *desalinize* (sea water so as to make it potable), *finalize* (the terms of a contract), *hospitalize* (the victims of a car crash for diagnosis and treatment), *hypnotize* (a person suffering from insomnia), *immunize* (a person against contagion), *industrialize* (a backward country), *institutionalize* (incorrigible delinquents), *moisturize* (dry skin), *optimize* (a computer programme), *pasteurize* (milk), *publicize* (company returns), *rationalize* (factory supply lines), *summarize* (documentary evidence), *transistorize* (receiving equipment), *visualize* (future possibilities). People who find these derivatives inelegant and unpleasant need not use them. Our vocabulary is so rich that there are always ready ways of evading them. In science and technology, however, they are indispensable and their number is increasing.

Throughout his long and busy life Noah Webster (1758–1843) was much concerned with reformed spelling. At his death the unsold copies of his Dictionary and its publishing rights were acquired by George and Charles Merriam. A new edition was prepared without delay by his son-in-law, Chauncey A. Goodrich of Yale University, to be followed in 1864 by the *American Dictionary of the English Language*, popularly known as *The Unabridged*, the work of Noah Porter, also of Yale. Meantime in London, on 5 and 19 November 1857, Richard Chenevix Trench, then Dean of Westminster, had read his two papers *On some deficiencies in our English dictionaries* to the Philological Society. These papers marked the inception of that great undertaking which produced in due time *The New English Dictionary on Historical Principles* (1884–1928), and its corrected re-issue which appeared under the title *The Oxford English Dictionary* with a Supplement in 1933.

Longevity, it has been observed, is the lexicographer's prerogative. The four editors of the *Oxford English Dictionary*, Sir James Murray (1837–1915), Henry Bradley (1845–1923), Sir William Craigie (1867–1957) and Charles Talbut Onions (1873–1965) all surpassed Dr Johnson's life-span of three quarters of a century. Their average age was well over eighty-four years and their lives covered a period of one century and a quarter. All four editors were interested in partial and gradual spelling reform.[1] Murray devoted his mature energies entirely to the Dictionary and found little time for any other kind of writing, but his joint-editors managed to produce various useful books. For instance, Bradley's *Making of English* (1904) soon became a classic, and Craigie's *English Spelling: Its Rules and Reasons* (1927) and his SPE Tract 59, *Some Anomalies of Spelling* (1942) have not been superseded as clear and authoritative statements about our traditional spelling. Craigie migrated to America in 1925 and inaugurated what might be regarded as the OED's transatlantic supplement, namely *A Dictionary of American English on Historical Principles* (1938–44). Onions took over *The Shorter Oxford English Dictionary* from William Little and made himself entirely responsible for its third and last edition in 1944. As his crowning achievement he compiled *The Oxford Dictionary of English Etymology* (1966) which has come to be regarded as the highest authority on word history throughout the whole English-speaking world.

By accepting a professorship in the University of Chicago and supervising postgraduate studies in lexicography, Craigie formed the living link between British and American traditions. He kept in touch with Dr William Allan Neilson who edited *Webster's New International Dictionary of the English Language*, second edition unabridged (sometimes called Webster II) in 1934, only one year after the publication of the corrected *Oxford English Dictionary* and its First Supplement. This Second Webster, actually the seventh in the series, was in some ways superior to the Third which appeared in 1961 under the editorship of Dr Philip Babcock Gove.

In the Preface and Explanatory Notes Dr Gove declared his intention to make Webster III the one comprehensive dictionary for 'the whole modern English-speaking world'. Unfortunately he made too many concessions to illiterate usage and, in the opinion of many discerning critics, this 'abrogation of authority'

---

[1] Murray's initial plans for the Dictionary allowed for the inclusion of alternative spellings. Those plans were so well conceived that neither he nor his co-editors ever had occasion to change them.

was wrongheaded and pointless. 'This anxiously awaited work that was to have crowned cisatlantic linguistic scholarship with a particular glory', wrote Wilson Follett, author of *Modern American Usage*, 'turns out to be a scandal and a disaster'.[1]

In this chapter we are concerned only with spelling and not with the prime functions of modern lexicography discussed by Follett and others in their caustic reviews. In spelling Gove certainly showed unprecedented permissiveness in recording such barbaric forms as *administrate, apostacy, caligraphy, demonstratable, exstacy, idiosyncracy, supercede* and *surprize* side by side with orthodox *administer, apostasy, calligraphy, demonstrable, ecstasy, idiosyncrasy, supersede* and *surprise* only because uneducated writers or careless printers had used these spellings somewhere in the United States. In England, too, such uses (or misuses) were not unknown. Henry Hallam, for example, overlooked the spelling *idiosyncracy* more than once in his *Introduction to the Literature of Europe* (1839). So, too, did Emile Victor Rieu in the erudite Introduction to his translation of *The Four Gospels* in Penguin Classics (1952). Surely these were mere typographical slips, both Hallam and Rieu being accomplished Greek scholars. Compositors are prone to make this error because *idiosyncrasy* happens to be the only compound in *-crasy* from Gk *krasis* 'mixture' as against numerous formations in *-cracy* – *aristocracy, autocracy, democracy, ergatocracy, ochlocracy, physiocracy, plutocracy, technocracy, theocracy*, not to forget the recent hybrid *meritocracy* – from Gk *kratos* 'power'. This orthographical distinction is all the more important and worth preserving. The wrong spelling distorts the distinctive meaning of *idiosyncrasy* as 'peculiar-together-mixing' of the elements in a man's make-up, personality or individuality; as, indeed, in Shakespeare's Brutus:

> *His life was gentle, and the elements*
> *So mix'd in him that Nature might stand up*
> *And say to all the world, ' This was a man!'*

[1] 'Sabotage in Springfield' in *The Atlantic*, January 1962, p. 73. Follett died in 1963 before completing his book on *Modern American Usage* which was eventually finished and published by an editorial team headed by Jacques Barzun.

It so happens that the adjectival derivatives of nouns in both
-cracy and *-crasy* end alike in *-cratic*. Today *idiosyncratic* is fast
becoming a vogue word in the writings of critics and reviewers
who have come to regard it as an elegant synonym for 'peculiar,
individualistic'.

Excessive deference to popular usage led Gove to place
nouns ending in *-logue* (Gk *-logos*, Lat. *-logus*, F *-logue*, Sp., Ital.
-logo, G *-log*) in three groups instead of one: (a) catalog *or*
catalogue; (b) analogue *also* analog, dialogue *also* dialog,
epilogue *also* epilog, monologue *also* monolog, prologue *also*
prolog; and (c) apologue, duologue (without alternatives).
This is palpably absurd.[1] Such an untidy tripartition can only be
justified on the ground of frequency. *Catalogue* 'list, register,
series' is in daily use in the world of books and commerce. It is
clearly the most frequently employed of all these words.
Apologue 'moral fable' remains archaic, recalling Æsop and the
talking beasts and birds of classical antiquity. *Duologue* 'conversation between two' is seldom heard anywhere because its
meaning is completely covered by *dialogue* 'conversation between
two persons or more' which many people vaguely associate
with the Greek prefix *di-* 'two, double' (whereas, in fact, the
first element is *dia-* 'through, across'). Oddly enough, *dialogue*
has greatly grown in frequency of use since the publication of
Webster III in 1961. It has indeed become a vogue word,
sounding more impressive than *negotiations* and more dignified
than *talks*. We now read of 'the dialogue between the Vatican
and the Kremlin' in the sense of 'prolonged diplomatic trans-
actions' or 'continuous exchange of views'.

It is hardly likely that any other great dictionary will follow
Webster III in this matter of aberrant spellings or that these
vagaries will have the slightest influence on the style rules of
reputable printing houses. In Britain the basic and unimpeachable authority is still APD or *The Authors' and Printers'*

----

[1] As stated in the Explanatory Notes (1. 7. 2) the conjunction *or*
denotes that the variants are of equal status, whereas the adverb *also*
denotes that the form following it is a 'secondary variant' which 'belongs
to standard usage and may for personal or regional reasons be preferred
by some'.

Dictionary by Frederick Howard Collins, 'a guide for Authors, Editors, Printers, Correctors of the Press, Compositors, and Typists. Approved by the Master Printers' and Allied Trades' Association of London, by the Edinburgh Master Printers' Association, by the Belfast Printing Trades Employers' Association, and by the Executive Committee of the London Association of the Correctors of the Press'.[1] Oxford has its own RCR or *Rules for Compositors and Readers*, first formulated by Horace Hart, Printer to the University, in 1893, and since that date frequently revised.

The time has surely arrived for Oxford and Springfield to come together and agree amicably on the spellings to be recommended to all. I say Oxford and Springfield because, in these days of greater and greater concentrations of power, including intellectual power, these two cities are the acknowledged centres of lexicological activity. The one-volume British dictionaries, Henry Cecil Wyld's *Universal English Dictionary*, Cassell's *English Dictionary*, Nuttall's *Standard Dictionary*, Chambers's *Twentieth Century Dictionary* and *The Penguin English Dictionary* all look to Oxford as their main source. Their compilers and revisers are eagerly awaiting OED's Second Supplement which is due to appear in 1974. The other large American dictionaries, *The New Century*, Funk and Wagnall's *Standard Dictionary* and *The Random House Dictionary* are far more independent, relying less and less on the latest Webster for their facts and information.

A DICTIONARY OF APPROVED SPELLINGS

Clearly, I repeat, the time has come for Oxford and Springfield to collaborate on equal terms in the production of a dictionary of approved spellings, not static and sacrosanct, but progressive and forward-looking, and subjected to (not too frequent) revisions. Such an authoritative work would ensure that reforms would be well-based and universal, not haphazard and regional.

[1] See G. H. Vallins, *Spelling*, revised by D. G. Scragg, Deutsch 1965, p. 151.

The editors of this glossary might indeed take a cue from Ann Arbor where Hans Kurath and Sherman McAllister Kuhn are editing the Michigan Middle English Dictionary under the joint sponsorship of both cis- and transatlantic 'scholarly organizations' including (in alphabetical order) the American Council of Learned Societies, the Clarendon Press, the Heckscher Foundation of Cornell University, the Modern Language Association of America, the Oxford English Dictionary, the Rockefeller Foundation, and the University of Michigan. Surely, if such an authentic guide were available, the future editors of Webster IV and the revised OED would be only too glad to abide by its rulings. One important contribution that this dictionary of approved spellings would make to linguistic efficiency would lie in the precise semantic differentiation between such divergent forms as (to mention only a few) *bogie* 'undercarriage', *bogy* 'goblin, bugbear'; *business* [bizniz] 'occupation, trade', *busyness* [bizinis] 'state of being busy'; *canvas* 'unbleached cloth of hemp or flax', *canvass* 'close examination, act of soliciting votes'; *chord* 'string of a musical instrument', *cord* 'thick string in general'; *clew* 'skein of thread or yarn', *clue* 'line of inquiry'; *daemon* 'genius, indwelling spirit', *demon* 'little devil'; *dis¹creet* 'circumspect, judicious', *discrete* 'not concrete'; *to douse* 'to extinguish', *to dowse* 'to search for water or minerals with a divining rod'; *enquiry* 'request', *inquiry* 'formal investigation'; *to ensure* 'to make safe', *to insure* 'to secure compensation by the payment of premiums'; *to forego* 'to go before', *to forgo* 'to go without'; *linage* [lainidʒ] 'lines of print', *lineage* [liniidʒ] 'ancestry, pedigree'; *mask* 'face covering', *masque* 'amateur dramatic entertainment with dances and disguises'; *naught* 'nothingness', *nought* 'the cipher 0'; *premises* 'land, buildings and appurtenances', *premisses* 'logical propositions'; *storey* 'floor', *story* 'narrative'; *suit* [sju:t] 'set of clothes, cards, etc.', *suite* [swi:t] 'set of attendants, rooms, etc.'.

The recognition of a global authority, based primarily on Anglo-American agreement, will in no way discourage or inhibit the zeal of potential reformers. After all, the realm of letters is a free and open domain. The wholehearted acceptance of one, and only one, standard pattern of written English for the whole world need not preclude experiments of various kinds in the immediate and distant future. It will enhance, rather than diminish, the value of such supplementary codes as shorthand, IPA and ITA: shorthand for reporters, the International Phonetic Alphabet for linguists, and the Initial Teaching Alphabet for infants.[1] Shorthand abbreviations are as old as civilization itself, but it was the publication in 1840 of Sir Isaac Pitman's *Phonography or Writing by Sound, being also a New and Natural System of Shorthand* that really marked the beginning of stenography as we know it.

THE SHAW ALPHABET

The Shaw alphabet owes much to Pitman's shorthand, and something to Arabic. It was launched in 1962 with the publication of the Penguin edition of *Androcles and the Lion*, dedicated to Sir James Pitman, Sir Isaac's grandson. George Bernard Shaw (1856–1950) provided money in his Will for the inauguration of a 'British Alphabet of at least forty letters' to be devised by a qualified phonetician. That alphabet has been since designed by Kingsley Read of Abbots Morton in Worcestershire. It consists, in fact, of forty-eight letters, four of which, those for *th, v, n* and *t*, also serve to denote the four most frequently occurring words: *the, of, and* and *to*. The special edition of *Androcles* (1962), already mentioned, has Shavian and orthographic texts on facing pages so that (to quote Pitman in his *Introduction*) the reader may 'notice from the comparisons that Shaw's alphabet is both more legible and one-third more economical in space than traditional printing, and this should lead to a great increase in reading speed'. No one, to be sure, can seriously question the second of these two claims because proof lies in simple measurement. Verso pages con-

---

[1] Nor should we forget, at this point, other systems like the deaf-and-dumb alphabet and the Morse code; and non-alphabetic systems like prehistoric and primitive pictograms, Chinese characters, musical notation, and sets of symbols used in logic, mathematics, genetics, physics, astronomy, chemistry, and other branches of science and technology.

taining the Shavian text have wide left-hand margins and recto pages have exceedingly narrow ones. But the first claim to greater legibility leaves one in grave doubt. The spacing of letters in the Shaw script is slightly uneven and very trying to the eyes. The italic letters are especially irritating. Unfortunately Shaw made frequent use of italics in his detailed and extensive stage directions. The italics in the conventional text, on the other hand, are exceptionally clear and attractive.

Many improvements have been made in the clarity and legibility of both roman and italic printing in recent decades. Place today's issue of *The Times* (or any other newspaper for that matter) side by side with that of forty years ago and these improvements will become at once apparent.[1]

The orthographic text of *Androcles and the Lion*, both roman and italic, is exceptionally clear and neat, and these qualities are still further enhanced by Shavian specialities – absence of inverted commas and minimal display of hyphens and apostrophes.

Will the Shaw alphabet remain in use? Kingsley Read is now editing a quarterly called *Shaw-Script* which contains essays, short stories and light verse presented in his special alphabet, but not one of the great daily or weekly newspapers has shown the slightest interest in the new venture.

THE NEW TEACHING ALPHABET

Meantime Sir James Pitman had been promoting another practical project whose aim was to help young children to learn to read more speedily. Here he was involved, not in a private venture in fulfilment of a quixotic bequest, but in a public enterprise undertaken with the formal support and approval of the then Minister of Education, Viscount Eccles.

The first trials were made in the early sixties. Their purpose

---

[1] A leading exponent and a tireless worker in this field was Stanley Morison (1889–1967), Typographical Adviser to the Cambridge University Press, member of *The Times* staff for over thirty years, and author of *Four Centuries of Fine Printing*.

was not to discard the inherited alphabet of twenty-four letters (not counting *j* and *v*), but to augment it by the addition of twenty letters, making forty-four in all, so that 'every English word could be read in one way only'.

ſhis iſ printed in an iniſhial teeℂhiŋ alfabet, ſhe purpos ov whiℂh iſ not, aſ miet bɛɛ suppœſd, tω reform our spelliŋ, but tω imprωv ſhe lerniŋ ov rɛɛdiŋ. it iſ intended ſhat when ſhe beginneɾ haſ aℂhɛɛvd ſhe iniſhial sucsess ov flωensy in ſhis speſhially ɛɛſy form, hiſ fuetueɾ progress ſhωd bɛɛ confiend tω rɛɛdiŋ in ſhe preſent alfabets and spelliŋſ ov ſhem œnly.

Notice, by the way, that this text is only approximately phonetic and that it presupposes a certain number of spelling pronunciations. *Initial* and *specially* are apparently to be enunciated as four syllables, not three: future progress is to be read as [fjutjuə prɔgres] not [fjuːtʃə prougres] as in RP.

After six years of experimentation in Britain, the United States and Australia, the sponsors of ITA could claim some measure of success in their endeavours to assist backward children to read. The inevitable switch from ITA to standard spelling at the age of seven years was found to be far less formidable than had been anticipated. Even the most sceptical observers had to concede that ITA was innocuous. While helping dull children from poor homes, it had not retarded bright ones from good homes since these had already learnt standard spelling before attending school at the age of five and had come to regard ITA lessons as merely amusing diversions. Some penetrating observers went further. They reminded Sir James Pitman that this schoolchildren's alphabet had a yet more profound significance for the future of English. In promoting ITA he was postponing his other more ambitious plans to reform English spelling 'for ten years, for twenty years, and perhaps for ever'.[1]

MARKS OF ABBREVIATION

You will have noticed that I follow current practice in writing ITA and not I.T.A., omitting periods as marks of abbreviation. Since the middle of the century some not unimportant changes have been made in what one might call the mechanics of spelling – in the uses of full stops, the apostrophe, inverted commas or quotes, hyphens, and capitals or uppercase letters. These changes have all formed part of a general movement towards greater clarity and simplicity. They are closely linked with those typographical improvements effected by Stanley Morison and others, and with that extensive re-organization of British newspapers achieved by a dynamic personality, Baron Roy Thomson of Fleet. More distantly they are linked with computer programming and with the rapid advance of automation.[2]

Let us assume that John Smith teaches chemistry in Leeds University and that he is a Commander of the Order of the British Empire, a Master of Arts, a Doctor of Science, and a Fellow of the Royal Society. In earlier editions of *The Commonwealth Universities Yearbook* you would find him recorded as John Smith, C.B.E., M.A., D.Sc., F.R.S. He appears in the current issue as John Smith CBE MA DSc FRS. Ten periods and four commas have been eliminated. Spacing is made to perform the function of punctuation. So, too, in his postal address –

Department of Chemistry

The University

Leeds 2

– there are no commas or full stops. The fact that the items in this address stand on separate lines renders punctuation redundant.

---

[1] In his younger days Pitman had seconded Mont Follick, Labour Member for Loughborough, in introducing a private member's Spelling Reform Bill into the House of Commons. This Bill was defeated (in a small house) by three votes on 11 March 1949.

[2] ENIAC, the first 'electronic numerical integrator and computer', was developed by a group of American scientists in 1942.

If, to save space, more than one item is printed on a line, commas are essential. Compare

> University of London Library
> Senate House
> Malet Street
> W.C.1

with

> University of London Library
> Senate House, Malet Street, W.C.1

In both cases the full stops are obligatory in W.C. to show clearly that this is the abbreviation for the name of a postal district (West Central).

It has long been a sensible custom to omit the stop after an abbreviation when its final letter is the same as that of the full form. So, in this book, I have written Lat. for Latin, but Gk for Greek. (I have also dispensed with the period after single initial capitals: E for English, IE for Indo-European. See the list of abbreviations on p. 9.) This custom is indeed so satisfactory that it will probably prevail, although some printing houses favour the extrusion of all marks of abbreviation. They prescribe Rev Dr, not Rev. Dr, as the abbreviated forms for Reverend Doctor.

The omission of the period after initial capitals has encouraged the creation of both acronyms like UNO and UNESCO, and alphabetisms like TLS [ti: el es] *The Times Literary Supplement* and STD [es ti: di:] 'Subscriber Trunk Dialling'. Because UNO happens to be homophonous with 'you know', more and more people use the ellipsis 'United Nations', treating it as a noun in the singular number in all official pronouncements.

The apostrophe or turned comma (Gk *apo-strophē* 'away turning') is also much less used whether as the mark of omission (as in *shant* for *shan't*, earlier *sha'n't*, for *shall not*) or as the specific mark of the genitive case (as in *St Albans* for *St Alban's*, earlier *St Albanes*). No one now writes *cou'dn't* or *wo'n't* as Swift rightly did for the reduced forms of *could not* and *wol not*. Shaw wrote *dont, didnt, havnt, shouldnt, weve* and *wont,* but, try as he would, he could not dispense with the turned comma in *I'd* and *I'll* for obvious reasons. Today the apostrophe is firmly established in all reduced forms of verbs:

> *not* abbreviated to *n't* in conjunction with all the twenty-four anomalous finites: an't, isn't, aren't, wasn't, weren't; haven't, hasn't, hadn't; don't, doesn't, didn't; shan't, shouldn't; won't, wouldn't; can't, couldn't; mayn't (rare), mightn't; mustn't; oughtn't; needn't; daren't; usedn't (rare);
> *is* and *has* abbreviated to *s* in he's, she's, it's, John's, Mary's, etc.;
> *am* to *m* in I'm;
> *are* to *re* in we're, you're, they're;
> *have* to *ve* in I've, we've, you've, they've;
> *had* to *d* in I'd, you'd, he'd, she'd, it'd, we'd, they'd;
> *will* and *shall* to *ll* in I'll, you'll, he'll, she'll, it'll, that'll, this'll, we'll, they'll;
> and *us* to *s* in let's (go).

Shaw's dilemma remains. Because the omission of the apostrophe will render many of the above forms ambiguous – ant, wont, cant, were, Id, shed, wed, Ill, hell, shell, well – it must of necessity be kept in all.

Elsewhere, however, the turned comma has gradually and silently vanished. It has gone from numerous aphetic forms like *bus* for *'bus* from *omnibus* 'for all' (F *voiture omnibus*, Sorbonne students' slang for *voiture pour tous*) and *'cello* for *violoncello* (Ital. diminutive of *violone* 'double-bass viol'). It is even now in the process of disappearing from many genitive plurals, especially those in which there is no clear notion of possession:

Women's Institute = Social institute for women living in country districts
Girls' School = School for girls
Trades' Union = Union of workers following various trades
Seven Years' War = War that lasted seven years
Teachers' Training College = College for the training of teachers
Pilgrims' Way = way or path followed by pilgrims

The Seven Years' War (1756–63) belongs to history, and this type of nominal phrase has now been almost completely superseded by the 'Seven-Year-War' type, or even 'Seven Year War' without a hyphen (OE *seofon gēara wīg*). So, for example, the Arab-Israeli June War of 1967 was referred to as the Six Day War in immediately subsequent reports.

In the late forties, to evade making any definite decision about the wanted or unwanted apostrophe, the title 'Teachers' Training College' was officially changed to 'Teacher Training College', but this was deemed by many to be even less satisfactory. Here was a nominal phrase of dubious grammaticality – an attributive gerund governing a preceding generic substantive. In 1964, therefore, this cumbersome phrase was finally abandoned in favour of the more honorific (though less strictly defining) 'College of Education'.

The prehistoric track from Alton to Canterbury was made in pagan antiquity, but it was later used by Christian pilgrims making their way to the shrine of St Thomas Becket. The best stretches lie along the ridge of the North Downs from Guildford to Chevening and they bear ornamental signposts inscribed PILGRIMS WAY without any disfiguring raised comma or apostrophe.

Two Royal Parks in Greater London retain an apostrophe in their official names, however frequently that mark may now be dropped in guidebooks or elsewhere. They are St James's [snt dʒeimziz] and Regent's Park. The latter was so named after the Prince Regent (1811–20) who subsequently reigned as King George IV (1820–30). To this Park 'The Regent's Street' led from Piccadilly although its northern section was later renamed Portland Place. 'The Regent's Street' has since become plain 'Regent Street' by the suppression of the definite article (p. 144) and the simplification of the double sibilant. In other place-names an untidy apostrophe has been tacitly abandoned within living memory: Earl's Court, for instance, now Earls Court, was the manor house of the de Veres, now Earls of Oxford, lords of the manor of Kensington from

[1] Cf. OE *prēora mīla gang* 'three-mile journey'. All genitive plurals ended in -*a* in OE, weakened to -*e* in ME, and reduced to zero in PE.

Domesday Book to the sixteenth century. St John's Wood, now St Johns Wood (at least as the name of the Underground Station) was once owned by the Knights of the Hospital of St John of Jerusalem. Golder's Green, now Golders Green, was formerly the property of the God(y)ere family. In other names the apostrophe has been omitted by the decree of the local authority: St Andrews in Fifeshire, St Bees in Cumberland, St Albans in Hertfordshire (mentioned above), St Helens in Lancashire and the Isle of Wight, St Davids in Pembroke, and St Ives in Cornwall and Huntingdonshire. And how about the appellations of department stores like Selfridges? Since the founder is no longer the sole proprietor of this huge corporation, the mark of possession has gone for ever.

INVERTED COMMAS

Monosyllabic *quotes* is a simpler term than *quotation marks* and it is a more precise term than *inverted commas* since only the initial commas are upside down. Are quotes really necessary? You will find no quotes in the King James Bible, in Shakespeare's First Folio, or in the authentic text of Shaw's plays. French and Russian manage without them, although they have recourse to other marks that are in some ways even less satisfactory.

All in all, quotes are so useful that they are not likely to disappear altogether. Nevertheless, they should always be employed carefully and sparingly.

Today single quotes are the normal ones. Double quotes are reserved only for a quotation within a quotation. This will surely stand as the style rule for tomorrow, however stubbornly some older houses hold out against it.

Quotes are used primarily to record the actual words of a speaker (direct speech): 'My dear Copperfield,' said Mr Micawber, 'yourself and Mr Traddles find us on the brink of migration, and will excuse any little discomforts incidental to that position.'

Quotes are used to indicate words taken from a published text: Autumn had come at last, that 'season of mists and mellow fruitfulness'.

Quotes are used for the title of an essay or article contributed to a journal or periodical whose name will normally stand in italics: L. P. Hartley, 'The Novelist's Responsibility', *Essays and Studies* XV (1962) p. 88.

In this book quotes are used to denote meaning whereas italics are employed to indicate a word named or referred to as a form, e.g., OE *wynn* 'joy'. This is a most useful convention in writings on linguistics. Apart from boldface type and various kinds of brackets — square brackets [ ] for phonetic, obliques or slants / / for phonemic, and braces { } for morphemic transcriptions, we can place a form on four distinctive planes of reference:

JOY	capital or uppercase
joy	lowercase
joy	italic
'joy'	within single quotes

In scientific writing quotes are used to warn the reader that a term is being employed in a technical or specialized sense:

> One cannot determine 'acceptability' by relating the passage concerned to the latest effusion of a fourth-rate novelist, but only by reference to the best conversational usage of educated speakers.

Here *acceptability*[1] is not used in its general sense of 'quality of being welcome or agreeable', but in its specialized philological meaning as a near-equivalent of *correctness* or *grammaticality*. It is unfortunate that some writers use (or misuse) these *specializing quotes* (as we may call them) far too lavishly. With a little more careful thought they could have found the right word. Instead of that, they have been content to put down the second-best word, and then, to salve their consciences, they have placed it within quotes. Some writers use specializing quotes deliberately – not one sentence without them – because they think that thereby they will impress the uninitiated.

[1] Note carefully that I am here 'naming' the word and I therefore italicize it instead of placing it within quotes. In that last sentence I put *naming* within quotes because I am using it in its philosophical sense. In the last sentence now I italicize it because I am referring to it.

HYPHENATION

Hyphens are essential in such phrases as *will-o'-the-wisp*, *stick-in-the-mud*, *go-between*, *ne'er-do-well*, and *happy-go-lucky*, but elsewhere every effort is being made to dispense with them. The hyphen, like the apostrophe, is suspect in the modern world. At its worst, people now say, it is a blemish in the line of clean print: at its best, it is a necessary nuisance.

The Encyclopaedia Britannica no longer issues a Year-Book but a Book of the Year. There are, in fact, three ways of writing the English equivalent of *Jahrbuch* and *jaarboek*, whereas in German and Dutch these compounds are invariable.

(a) *open*   year book
(b) *hyphened*   year-book
(c) *solid*   yearbook

At present all three styles are current in book titles:
(a) The International Year Book and Statesmen's Who's Who
(b) The Statesman's Year-Book
(c) Yearbook of the United Nations

Clearly (c) is the neatest. It accords completely with its German and Dutch equivalents, cited above. It is a tatpurusha type of compound that has been in use in English for hundreds of years, written solid by Anglo-Saxon scribes.

A language may hold within itself formative powers which may expand or contract in use, or even lie dormant for centuries. The *yearbook* type of compound, consisting of noun + noun, determinans + determinatum, the first component modifying the second, is inherent in all the Germanic languages, but it remains undeveloped in Romance. A Frenchman says, not *anlivre*, but *annuaire*. He uses a derivative instead of a compound as, indeed, we can if we so desire. Our horticultural yearbook is entitled *Gardener's Annual*. In both English and French, of course, *annual* and *annuaire* are substantivized adjectives agreeing with the nouns *book* and *livre* understood. The official title of the French edition of the Yearbook of the United Nations is *Annuaire des Nations Unies*.

Parasynthetic agent nouns *(beekeeper, bridgebuilder, landowner, townplanner)* and parasynthetic compound adjectives *(factfinding, laboursaving, peaceloving, timeconsuming)* are now printed solid. Phrasal verbs *(break through, flare up, hang over, take over)* are now printed open, but, when used as nouns, hyphens are sometimes introduced for the sake of clarity. *Breakthrough* and *hangover* can be printed solid without question, but not so obviously *flareup* and *takeover*. This particular problem remains unsolved.

Meanwhile the three adverbs of time – *to-day, to-night* and *to-morrow* – hyphened thus in OED (1909) and SOED (1933) – were printed solid in Webster III (1961) and the latest COD (1964). *Today, tomorrow* and *tonight* will be the only forms in future. When the urban districts of Kingston-on-Thames and Richmond-on-Thames were promoted to the status of Greater ondon Boroughs in 1964 no one found occasion to query the tacit changes of name to Kingston upon Thames and Richmond upon Thames. At the same time, as an unobserved ripple in the rising tide of dehyphenation, Shakespeare's birthplace was silently renamed Stratford upon Avon.

PREFERENCE FOR LOWERCASE

Do you write *Biblical* or *biblical, Cockney* or *cockney, Neo-Platonic, neo-platonic* or *neo-Platonic*? 'When in doubt, prefer lowercase' is simple advice summarizing current custom. Dutch has finally abandoned the capitalization of common nouns. Will Germany follow her neighbour's lead? A glance at Shakespeare's First Folio of 1623 will show how lavish (though inconsistent) Heminge and Condell were with their sprinkling of capitals and italics, but even they were surpassed by the Augustans who were yet more profligate in their display of scribal embellishments:

First follow NATURE, and your Judgment frame
By her just Standard, which is still the same:
Unerring Nature, still divinely bright,
One *clear, unchang'd*, and *Universal* Light,
Life, Force, and Beauty, must to all impart,
At once the *Source*, and *End*, and *Test* of *Art*.

Compare the typographical complexity of these well-known verses from Pope's *Essay on Criticism* (1711) with the simplicity of the concluding lines of Eliot's *Little Gidding* (1942):

> And all shall be well and
> All manner of thing shall be well
> When the tongues of flame are in-folded
> Into the crowned knot of fire
> And the fire and the rose are one.

CHAPTER 3

New Words

As OUR daily lives become more sophisticated, so names for new things inevitably multiply, and as our intellectual pursuits grow more highly developed, so names for various kinds and degrees of abstractions proliferate endlessly.[1] Thousands of these new terms are, it is true, used only by specialists; and yet, thanks to mass media of communication, many highly specialized terms pass swiftly into general use.

Some new words, like *spoof* and *blurb*, were created by one man. In 1889 the British comedian Arthur Roberts named and invented that card game *spoof* which later came to typify hoaxing and humbug in general. In 1907 the American journalist Gelett Burgess hit upon the idea of calling the publisher's 'puff' or commendation, often printed on a book-jacket, the *blurb*. Other new words, like *hormone* and *vitamin*, were taken from Greek and Latin to denote hitherto unknown entities. These entities were indeed suspected but never identified by Darwin and Huxley. Hormone is the slightest modification (by adding final e) of *hormôn*, the present participle of the Greek verb *hormáein* 'to set in motion, excite, stimulate'. Hormones are those glandular secretions in the blood stream which stimulate bodily organs to action.[2] They were so designated by Dr Ernest Starling who referred to them in *The Lancet* on 5 August 1905 as 'these chemical messengers, or hormones as we might call them'. Earlier in this same year Dr Casimir Funk announced his discovery of those vital constituents of food which he labelled *vitamines* (Lat. *vita* 'life' + *amine*

---

[1] 'No language is so sophisticated as English – it is abstracted to death'. Samuel Beckett, *Essay on Joyce* (1929).

[2] OED Supplement 1933 s.v. *hormone*.

'ammonia component'). Later, when he learnt that these life-giving constituents were not true amines after all, he suppressed the final -*e* in token of acknowledged error! Today vitamins are known to form a series of organic substances essential to normal metabolism. Distinguished by capital letters from A to X, they frequently appear on commercial television.

In the spring of 1928 a tiny speck of something floated through an open window of St Mary's Hospital, Paddington. It might have been any window of that extensive building, but 'by chance or nature's changing course' that same tiny particle, the spore of a common green mould or mildew, drifted through the open window of Dr Alexander Fleming's research laboratory and it settled on one of his culture plates. It quickly grew among the staphylococci bacteria already planted there, destroying those it touched. Clearly it was a potent organism hitherto unknown to man. Dr Fleming called it *penicillin*. It was not long before this antibiotic was being produced on a worldwide scale as a therapeutic drug of great power against many forms of disease.

Only seven years later, in 1935, Dr Gerhard Domagk, a pathologist experimenting at Wuppertal in the Rhineland, proclaimed another discovery that marked the greatest single advance in chemotherapy ever made. He called the substance *prontosil*. It was to be the precursor of all the sulphonamides.

In the same year 1935 that plastic material of many purposes was invented which we call *polythene*, although the group of ICI chemists who then first put it on the market named it *poly-eth-el-ene*, a polymer of *ethelene* or *ether-yl-ene*, from Gk *aithēr* 'upper air', *hýlē* 'wood, material', and -*ēnē*, a feminine patronymic suffix. Are *polythene, melamine, neoprene, polyester, polystyrene* and other names just technical terms that will pass away as the particular plastics they denote are superseded by others of yet greater utility? No one can be sure. At the moment these trade names are universal. They already belong to the world vocabulary of science (Chapter 4).

Again, take the neologism *cybernetics*. This was concocted in 1942 as a blanket word (from Gk *kubernētēs* 'steersman') by Dr Norbert Wiener, a mathematician in the Massachusetts Institute of Technology, to cover all systems of automatic control and communications in both animals and machines, including computers, thermostats and photoelectric sorters.

And what about *sputnik?* This is pure Russian, and it came into English on 4 October 1957 when Sir Bernard Lovell, Director of Jodrell Bank Experimental Station in Cheshire, reported the launching of the first man-made satellite from the spacedrome near Baikonur. Weighing 180 pounds, this artificial satellite or sputnik circled the globe in 95 minutes. It marked the beginning of the Space Age.

LOANWORDS

We call *sputnik* a borrowed word or *loanword*.[1]

It is an old Russian word meaning 'travelling companion' from *s-* 'with', *put* 'way', and *-nik*, an agent suffix. This agent suffix *-nik* also lives in Yiddish, as in *kibbutznik* a member of a *kibbutz* 'gathering, community dwelling'. In the early sixties this suffix gave rise to *beatnik*,[2] a member of the *beat* or *beaten* generation (also addicted to *beat* or rhythmic music). Then in America it produced *peacenik* and *straightnik* and many other playful formations in *-nik* — perhaps only a passing fashion.

Closer contacts with Russia in recent years have led to an augmented use of many old terms relating to the landscape— *steppe* 'treeless grassland', and *tundra* (of Lapp origin) 'arctic plain'; terms relating to transport and travel – *verst* 'Russian mile', *droshky* 'low open carriage', *tarantass* 'long springless carriage', and *troika* 'three-horse team driven abreast'; to music – *balalaika* 'triangular guitar'; to home life – *borscht* 'cabbage and beetroot soup', *samovar* 'self-boiler' and so 'tea urn', *vodka* 'rye brandy' a hypocoristic derivative of *voda* 'water'; to government – *soviet* 'council', *duma* 'thought' and so 'deliberative assembly' (before 1917), *bolshevik* 'member of the greater or majority party', and *Kremlin* (of Tatar origin) 'citadel'. We hear frequent references to the party newspaper *Pravda* 'truth', to the official government journal *Izvestia* 'news', and to the evening paper *Večernaya Moskva*.

[1] *Loanword* is itself a loan-translation or *calque* from G *das Lehnwort*.

[2] The concept of a 'beaten generation' was popularized by the Canadian-born novelist Jean-Louis Lefris de Kérouac (b. 1922).

Today our debt to France for borrowed words is as great as ever, and English influence on French is even greater.[1] Cultural and linguistic interchange has operated continuously for the greater part of a millennium; ever since, in fact, the year 1002 when Emma, daughter of Duke Richard I of Normandy, married King Æthelred of England and by him became the mother of Edward the Confessor. Since then French influence has continued without intermission throughout the centuries, though operating with greatly varying degrees of intensity. It was exceptionally potent immediately after the Norman Conquest of 1066 and it remained strong throughout the Age of the Crusades (1095–1270) when French was the first language of Christendom. It was powerful after 1660 when the Merry Monarch looked to Louis Quatorze as the *arbiter elegantiae* of western civilization. It is now most evident in technical terms relating to dress and fashion, cuisine and viniculture, politics and diplomacy, drama and literature, art and ballet. Look at this week's quality newspapers, the *Observer* and the *Sunday Times*, or at this month's ladies' magazines, *Queen* and *Vogue*, and you will probably find an average of one italicized Gallicism on every page. Not all readers, it is true, are fully aware of the precise *nuances* conveyed by all the French expressions they encounter in such newspapers and magazines nor are they in the least concerned with their linguistic origins: that *contretemps*, for instance, is really a pass or thrust in the noble art of fencing made 'against time', inopportunely, or at the wrong moment; and that *aplomb* (from the builder's term *à plomb*) signifies 'according to the plummet or plumb-line'. *Aplomb* 'self-possession' is, you will agree, an enviable quality always and everywhere, and so in their different ways are *insouciance* 'careless indifference', *nonchalance* 'cool unconcern', and *bonhomie* 'good-natured geniality'. A *brouhaha* is not the same as a *fracas*. The former applies to the public clamour attending some sensational event, the latter denotes a quick fight or sudden disturbance. A *coup* unqualified is always a *coup d'état* or 'violent change of government', although other sorts of *coup*

[1] See René Étiemble, *Parlez-vous franglais?* Paris, Gallimard 1964.

may enliven our conversation, whether *coup de grâce* 'finishing stroke', or *coup d'oeil* 'rapid glance', or *coup de théâtre* 'dramatic turn of events'. *Avant-garde* signifies high praise among those writers and artists whose desire above all things is to be 'with it' and 'in it', and to climb on to the most fashionable bandwagon regardless of the circus parade's destination. The avantgardists are ever busy blazing new trails: they dread being called 'squares'. In Paris a *boutique* is any kind of stall or booth, but in London it denotes any shop dealing specifically in ready-to-wear clothes and accessories. In modern Athens a shop is *magazí* like F *magasin*, but in ancient Athens a shop or store was *apotēhkē*, the etymological antecedent of *boutique*. A *bibliothēkē* was a bookcase in ancient Athens, just as *une bibliothèque* signifies a library in modern Paris, where *une librairie* is a bookshop. The latter is indeed fashionable in Soho and Mayfair, but the second component of *bibliothèque* lives in *discothèque* [diskou'tek] a *cabaret* where one can dance to canned music into the small hours. In spite of efforts to revive *questionary* [kwes tʃənəri][1] as an acceptable anglicization of *questionnaire* [kɛstjɔ'nɛə] the latter persists stubbornly in use to indicate 'a series of formal questions, usually printed with spaces left for the answers, devised to obtain statistics, opinions, and information generally on some specific subject'. The older word *interrogatory* is now quite obsolete in this sense. This preference for French forms and French pronunciations is not, I think, affectation. It is surely to be regarded as a manifestation of commendable *joie de vivre* on the part of the younger generation to whom the most civilized city in the world is ever *ville lumière* and its matchless cathedral is ever *Notre Dame*. As for actorless sound and light drama, it is just plain *son et lumière*.[2]

[1] *Questionary* is not, as is often stated, a recent anglicization. It was used in Tudor days. See OED, s.v. *questionary*, sb² *rare*.

[2] In 1952 Paul Robert-Houdini watched the effects produced by a violent thunderstorm on the appearance of the Château de Chambord in the Loire valley. It occurred to him that historical events might be re-enacted by the interplay of sound and light on an ancient building as background. By means of a computer the sound and light tracks of recordings might be synchronized electronically. The first successful *son et lumière* productions in England were given at Greenwich Palace in 1957.

C

French stress is persistently preserved in the pronunciation of scores of words like *ama'teur, baga'telle, ba'nal, bi'zarre, ca'chet, connoi'sseur, cri'tique, doctri'naire, fa'çade, fi'nesse, ma'cabre, pres'tige* and *tech'nique;* but stress remains remarkably unstable in *garage* in spite of the fixity of final stress in other fairly recent derivatives in Lat. *-āticum* like *camou'flage, entou'rage, espio'nage, me'nage* and *persi'flage.* A derivative of *gare* 'railway station' (from OHG *warōn* 'to guard'), *garage* is etymologically any building appended or annexed to a *gare* or 'place of protection'.[1] *Garage* is now almost universal, and yet Sir James Murray, who compiled the g-fascicles for the OED in 1897, had never heard of it. Indeed, according to the 1933 Supplement, its first recorded instance in English appeared in an article in the *Daily Mail* for 11 January 1902 describing the new 'garage' built by Mr Harrington Moore, secretary of the Automobile Club, to house eighty cars in Queen Victoria Street. Today many pronunciations of *garage* are current, ranging from [ga'rɑːʒ] rhyming with *barrage*, with stress still unfronted, to [garidʒ] rhyming with *marriage*. Meantime the French pronunciation [rənɛ'sãs] is being restored to the historical *Renaissance*, thus distinguishing it usefully from Latin-derived *renascence* [ri'nasns] denoting 'rebirth' in a general sense.[2]

Since 1945 German loanwords have been few. Of all the Nazi terms that were current before that year – *Luftwaffe, Reichswehr, Schutzstaffel, Sturmabteilung,* and countless others, *Lebensraum* 'space for living', *Blitz* and *Blitzkrieg* are among the few to

---

[1] Most other European languages have forms related to our *station* (Ital. *la stazione,* Sp. *la estación,* Russ. *stantsia*), but G *Bahnhof* 'rail court' is a notable exception. In Czechoslovakia a bus or coach stop is *stanice* and a railway station is *nádraží,* a derivative of *dráha* 'track'. In England a *bus stop* may be placed anywhere on a highway, but a *bus station* is found only in towns and cities where it is an enclosed yard with stands and bays. This distinction arose tacitly in the thirties when cross-country coach routes were revived.

[2] Matthew Arnold in *Culture and Anarchy* (1869) was largely responsible for confusing these doublets and for applying the Latin variant to the historical rebirth – 'the great movement which goes by the name of the Renascence', adding in a note: 'I have ventured to give to the foreign word Renaissance an English form'.

survive.[1] Today German influence, though slight, is subtle. It has a way of operating through Pennsylvania Dutch (which is German) but conclusive evidence is seldom forthcoming. *Unclear* and *meaningful* echo *unklar* and *bedeutungsvoll* (or *sinnvoll*). *Dumb* in the sense of 'stupid' is surely G *dumm*. 'Dumb' is G *stumm:* 'deaf and dumb' is *taufstumm*. *Fresh* in the sense of 'cheeky, amorously impudent' has surely arisen from association with G *frech*. 'Fresh' is G *frisch:* 'wet paint' as a warning notice is *frisch gestrichen*. One assumes that 'classless society', 'inferiority complex' and 'wishful thinking' are close renderings of *die klassenlose Gesellschaft, der Minderwertigkeits-komplex* and *das Wunschdenken*, but these remain assumptions still. Psychological *empathy*, like theological *charisma*, has become a vogue word. It may imply much more than *sympathy* (G *das Mitgefühl*), having the deeper connotation of *die Einfühlung* 'the power of projecting one's personality into, and so fully understanding, the object of contemplation'. So arises a new verb *empathize*. By strength of thought one can *empathize* with people and situations. A *separate* in the sense of 'offprint' looks like an adaptation of G *das Separatum*, now used in scientific circles for older *Sonderabdruck*. 'I wouldn't know' as an apologetic avowal of ignorance sounds like a translation of *ich wüsste nicht*, but who can prove it? A recent importation is *kibitzer* (from Yiddish *Kibitz* for G *Kiebitz* 'lapwing, peewit') strictly 'a back-watcher at a game of cards' and then a busybody or 'any meddlesome person who gives advice gratuitously'.

The period of Italian influence was also short, coinciding approximately with Shakespeare's lifetime (1564–1616). Then and afterwards, Italian became the universal language of music. Today the names of voices and parts, of performers, instruments, forms of composition and technical directions – all are Italian. Many technical directions are now used in transferred senses: *adagio* 'slow, in a leisurely manner', from *ad agio* 'at ease'; *allegro* 'lively, gay', from Lat. *alacer* 'brisk'; *andante* 'moderately slow and even', from the present participle of *andare* 'to

[1] 'The six-day war, which Israel began on the morning of June 5, was a classic example of a blitzkrieg.' *The Times Review of the Year*, 29 December 1967.

walk'; *crescendo* 'gradually increasing in volume' from the present participle of *crescere* 'to grow'; *pizzicato* 'played by plucking the strings' from the past participle of *pizzicare* 'to pinch'; *rallentando* 'gradually slowing down', from the present participle of *rallentare* 'to slacken'; and *staccato* 'in sharply detached manner', from the past participle of *staccare*, aphetic form of *distaccare* 'to detach'. Centuries are numbered from their opening year so that *trecento*, short for *mil trecento*, refers to the fourteenth century in Italian art and literature – the age of Dante, Petrarch and Boccaccio – and *quattrocento, cinquecento* and *seicento* denote the three subsequent centuries. *Trecentista* 'fourteenth century artist' is now sometimes anglicized to *trecentist*. *Risorgimento* 'resurrection', the title of Cavour's newspaper founded in 1847, refers strictly and exclusively to the movement (1750–1870) for liberation and unification. *Aggiornamento* 'bringing up to date' refers strictly and exclusively to that modernization of church government which marked the enlightened papacy of John XXIII (1958–63). *Trampolino* 'springboard' has given us the acrobat's *trampolin*.

New words from Spanish are few, but they have their special flavour: *bonanza* 'goodness, prosperity' especially in mining and farming, and then in general any kind of 'spectacular windfall' and any source of 'superabundant wealth'; *mañana* 'tomorrow' with a subaudition (unshared by Port. *amanha*, Ital. *domani* and F *demain*) of an inscrutable and utterly unpredictable future. A prisoner is *incommunicado* (spelt in Spanish with a single *m*) when he is denied all contact with the outside world, and a peasant is *decamisado* if he has no shirt. He is, in fact, a *have-not* – an expression that harks back to Cervantes.[1]

By way of California, New Mexico and Texas we have obtained *cigar, lasso, mustang, pueblo* and *rodeo*.

From Chinese we have acquired *sampan*, from *san* 'three' and *pan* 'board', a small boat propelled by a single skull over the

---

[1] Dos linages solos hay en el mundo, como decía una agüela mia, que son el tenir y el no tenir. 'There are only two families in the world, as my grandmother used to say, the haves and the have-nots.' *Don Quixote* II 20.

stern; and *tycoon*, from *ta* 'great' and *kiun* 'prince' by way of Japanese. From Japanese direct we have *karate*, a new skill in weaponless self-defence superseding *judo* and *jujitsu; bushido*, from *bu* 'military', *shi* 'man' and *do* 'dogma', the code of honour and morals evolved by the *samurai; banzai*, from *ban* 'ten thousand' and *zai* 'year', meaning elliptically 'ten thousand years of life to you' an imperial greeting and a cheer; *no* 'classical drama with dance and song'; and *kabuki* 'popular drama with music and stylized acting'; not to forget *kimono* 'wide-sleeved robe fastened by a broad sash at the waist'. Geographers now speak of a *tsunami*, from *tsu* 'harbour' and *nami* 'wave' to describe a Pacific Ocean wave produced by a submarine eruption, and fruiterers now call Japanese tangerines *satsumas*.

Jihad, Islam's holy war against unbelievers, was formally proclaimed by the Arabs in 1967 when the *Knesset* or Israeli parliament acted swiftly and Jewish soldiers, of whom many were children of the *kibbutzim*, won the six-day war in the month of June.

Apartheid, the Afrikaans or Cape Dutch form of *apart-hood*, applied first to racial segregation in South Africa, was extended northwards into Rhodesia in 1964 and was later used with reference to the separation of Greeks and Turks in Cyprus. Swedish *ombudsman* came in with the appointment in 1966 of an independent arbiter between government and individuals as in the Scandinavian countries and New Zealand, although he was officially designated a Parliamentary Commissioner for Administration. The Finnish steam bath or *sauna* is now popular and new forms of dress include an Eskimo jacket with a hood called an *anorak* and Eskimo fur-lined gumboots of sealskin called *mukluks*. A woman's two-piece swim suit or *bikini* is so called after an atoll of that name in the Marshall Islands.

COMPOSITION AND DERIVATION

New words can be invented, they can be borrowed from another language, or they can be formed by those morphological processes which happen to be active within a speech community at any particular time. German and Dutch, like ancient Greek, make greater use of composition (or compounding) than derivation (or affixation). French and Spanish, on the other hand, like classical Latin, prefer derivation to composition. Present-day English is making fuller use of both composition and derivation than at any previous time in its history.

When free forms are joined to make primary compounds like *pinpoint, cloverleaf* and *roadhouse* – to take three at random – it is important to observe that usage alone determines meaning. The verb *pinpoint* signifies 'to locate precisely'. One can pinpoint a target for bombing, a problem for solving, an error for eliminating, or, to quote a technical journal, one can 'pinpoint promising engineers by psychometric methods'. To motorists a *cloverleaf* is a well-defined road pattern at the intersection of highspeed motorways in which there are no right-hand turns. A *roadhouse* is not any wayside dwelling, but an inn, dance hall, tavern or night club located on a main road in a country district. The current meanings of these syntactic compounds, though restricted by time and custom, are readily deducible, but not the implications of hyphenated asyntactic compounds like *baby-sit* and *trigger-happy*. No one talked about *baby-sitting* in the nineteenth century when ordinary domestic help was cheap and available. A *trigger-happy* fellow is not only one who shoots on the slightest provocation but also, in a transferred sense, one who is aggressively and wantonly critical of the actions of others.

Affixation is now extremely active. Take, for instance, the prefixes *inter-, mini-* and *para-*. It is not easy to keep track of new derivatives. Some, it is true, are probably ephemeral: they will not survive this decade, let alone this century. *Inter -* 'between, among, in the midst of, reciprocally' enjoyed a limited use in sixteenth-century English. You will find *interdiction, intergatory* (for *interrogatory*), *interlude, intermission* and *interpret* in Shakespeare. It was, however, characteristic of eighteenth-century attitudes that Jeremy Bentham (in his *Introduction to Principles of Morals and Legislation* xvii 25) felt himself bound to apologize for creating a new derivative: 'The word *international*, it must be acknowledged, is a new one; though, it is hoped, sufficiently analogous and intelligible. It is calculated to express, in a more significant way, the branch of that law which goes commonly under the name of the law of nations'. By *sufficiently analogous* Bentham meant 'having enough models or parallels' among derivatives already in use. Today his new creation is current in all western languages. Besides the International Monetary Fund and the International Code of Signals, there is the International Labour Organization, a specialized agency of the United Nations. But monosyllabic *World* is preferred as an attributive noun in World Health Organization, and the International Bank for Reconstruction and Development is now briefly referred to as *World Bank* (without the definite article). International Student Service (ISS) has become World University Service (WUS). The organization to promote interconfessional unity is called World Council of Churches.

Elsewhere *inter-* is a fully living prefix. It is used to form not only Latin derivatives like *interconfessional* just mentioned, *intercontinental, interdenominational, interdisciplinary,* and *interdepartmental,* but also countless hybrids like *intercounty* and *interstate.* Financiers offer 'interbank facilities' and librarians arrange 'interlibrary loans'. Sociologists discuss *interclass, interfamily, intergroup* and even *interfaith* relationships.

Mini- is also a fully living prefix, but its advent is recent. Historically it is an abbreviation of Ital. *miniature,* an illumination painted in *minium* or red lead in a medieval manuscript. Vellum being precious, such manuscript illuminations were often exquisitely small. Was it surprising, therefore, that people associated the *min-* of *minium* and *miniatura* with the *min-* of Lat. *minor* and *minimus*? In 1935 the Eavestaff Minipiano was registered as a trade name, but it was not until 1960, when the British Motor Corporation produced its Mini Minor car, that *mini-* burst out into sudden blaze and brought forth *mini-bus* (revival of older *minibus*), *mini-cab* (small London taxi 1963), *mini-car, mini-cam* (miniature camera), *mini-budget* (interim estimate 1966) and even *mini-by-pass* (1967).

No less prolific is Greek *para-* 'beside' seen in *parable* 'throwing alongside, comparison', *paradigm* 'showing side by side, pattern (of inflexions)', *paradox* 'side opinion, conflicting with accepted notions', *parallel* 'alongside one another', *paraplegia* 'side striking, partial paralysis', and *paraselene* 'mock moon'.[1] From the physical concept of 'beside' it has now developed the meaning 'amiss, irregular', sometimes implying altered form or modification. The sedative and hypnotic drug *paraldehyde* is a polymer of aldehyde, produced by the polymerization of acetaldehyde with sulphuric acid. *Parapsychology* is concerned with psychic phenomena existing beside psychology proper – psi phenomena of extrasensory perception, including clairvoyance, telepathy, psychokinesis and precognition. *Paramedical* assistants are technicians and pharmacists serving the medical profession in a secondary or supplementary capacity. When philologists talk of *paralinguistics* they have in mind those speech features which lie beside and beyond segmental phonemes and suprasegmental prosodemes – whisper, breathiness, huskiness, creak, falsetto, resonance, and all those throat noises or 'voiced pauses' made by speakers when thought lags behind articulation.

Other frequently used prefixes are Greek *anti-, eu-, hyper-, hypo-* and *neo-;* Latin *ex-, sub-, super-, supra-* and *ultra-;* and native *near-, off-* and *self-. Anti-,* pronounced [antai] in North America, may even function as an adjective: 'We are all *anti*'. In a democratic society every ideology has its healthy pros and cons. Communism ineluctably evokes *anticommunism,* and nationalism *antinationalism.* The internal combustion engine has limitations that call for countermeasures: hence *antifreeze, antiknock* and *antinoise.* In medical practice *antibiotics* save life. The unattractive hybrid *antibody* is irreplaceable.

Meantime suffixes also multiply: *-ie* in *clippie* 'bus conductress', *deepie* 'three-dimensional film', *quickie* 'anything hastily done, whether a quick movie made to satisfy the requirements of the Films Quota Act, a trivial short story, or a quick drink'; *-(e)ry* in *adhocery* 'process of evading problems by appointing

[1] To be distinguished from that other *para-* seen in *parachute, parapet* and *parasol* from the imperative of Ital. *parare* 'to parry, ward off, protect'. A medical practitioner who parachutes to patients in remote areas is a *paradoctor,* and a soldier trained to land by parachute in enemy territory is a *paratrooper.*

ad hoc committees', *eatery* (jocular nickname for a restaurant coined by P. G. Wodehouse), *electric circuitry, gadgetry, gimmickry, rocketry, summitry* 'oganization of conferences at the highest levels'; *-ette* in *flannelette, leatherette, plushette* (names of imitation materials), *launderette* 'laundromat, commercial laundry with coin-operated machines', *maison(n)ette* 'part of a house rented separately, not necessarily, like a flat, on one level', *pramette* 'small perambulator or baby carriage', and *sleeperette* 'sleeping berth on an airliner'.

Expressive derivatives in *-manship* and *-ness* deserve special mention. OE *manscipe* rendered Lat. *humanitas*. In the west country *manship* still means 'manliness, courage'. *Workmanship* is found first recorded in the fourteenth century, *horsemanship* in the sixteenth, *craftsmanship* in the seventeenth, *seamanship* in the eighteenth, and *chairmanship* in the nineteenth. In the twentieth century it is the mock-serious social studies of Stephen Potter – *Gamesmanship, Lifemanship* and *One-Upmanship* – that have given these parasynthetic compounds their wide vogue. In 1956 Adlai Stevenson applied *brinkmanship* to that perilous species of diplomacy which advances to the brink of war without actually shooting. Among the more interesting recent formations in *-ness* are *divisiveness* and *permissiveness;* cold *calculatingness, forehandedness, forthputtingness, givenness, outgoingness, togetherness* and *wideawakeness.*

Turning now to new adjectival derivatives, we find a considerable increase in *-y* forms (OE *-ig* as in *hungrig, windig* and *wordig*). Since 1800 this suffix has tended to suggest lighthearted triviality as in *balmy, barmy, batty* 'having bats in the belfry', *bossy, cushy, dotty* 'off one's dots', and *squiffy* 'slightly intoxicated'. In a letter to Thomas Moore on 31 October 1815 Byron listed the eight stages of conviviality or togetherness: 'Like other parties of the kind, it was first silent, then talky, then argumentative, then disputatious, then unintelligible, then altogethery, then inarticulate, and then drunk.'[1] Both *talky* and *altogethery* were, of course, Byronic

[1] Quoted by John D. Jump in *Essays and Studies,* New Series X 1968 p. 69.

nonce-words.[1] The latter sounds delightfully modern, anticipating those numerous epithets which, however informal and slangy, will probably rise in status because they are so vividly expressive: *cagey* 'unapproachable, shrewdly circumspect' like a bird or animal in a cage; *chancy* 'uncertain, risky' (but in Scottish *chancy* means 'lucky' echoing F *Bonne chance!* 'Good luck to you!'); *choosy* 'hard to please, particular, fastidious'; *edgy* 'irritable, with nerves on edge'; *kinky* 'bizarre, with a mental twist or kink'; *peppy* 'energetic, full of pep or pepper'; *snooty*, 'superciliously contemptuous, looking down one's snoot or snout'; and *trendy* 'following the very latest trends in fashion'.

In the early sixties the suffix *-wise* crossed the Atlantic from Madison Avenue where it had probably been influenced by G *-weise* in such familiar expressions as *haufenweise* and *massenweise*. By using these new derivatives in *-wise* like *advertisementwise* 'by way of advertising', *fashionwise* 'with an eye to fashion', *manpowerwise* 'in terms of man power', *moneywise* 'from a financial point of view', *percentagewise* 'reckoning on a percentage basis' and *publicitywise* 'with a view to public relations', we can often reduce a cumbrous phrase to one word. If we read (*Sunday Times* 21 May 1967) that a certain destination is 'jetwise four hours near' we gather at once from the context that we can, if we wish, fly by jet-propelled plane from London to the Sheraton-Malta hotel in four hours. The statement is brief, but it really has little else to recommend it. On the whole these fashionable derivatives in *-wise* are too vague and imprecise to merit survival.

DIFFERENTIATING SUFFIXES

Never before has our language generated so many differentiating suffixes to convey subtle nuances of signification. They present a challenge to careful speakers and writers since their right use is essential to precise communication. *Elemental* and *elementary*, for instance, are synonymous epithets in so far as

---

[1] In OED the earliest instance of *talky* is cited from Carlyle's *History of Frederic the Great*, Book IV, 1862.

they both relate to first things, but whereas *elemental* refers to the four ancient Empedoclean elements of earth, water, air and fire, or their manifestations in nature, *elementary* is applied to elements in general as first principles or rudiments. *Emergence* and *emergency* are synonyms since they both relate to the act or process of coming up out of an enclosed space, but whereas *emergence* refers to this action simply and specifically, an *emergency* is a sudden juncture or situation coming up and demanding immediate action. Again, *continuance, continuation* and *continuity* all relate to the act or state of enduring or remaining in existence, but whereas *continuance* refers to enduring intransitively, *continuation* implies resumption in a transitive sense, whereas *continuity* describes the state or quality of being continuous. These, and scores of others, are well-established discriminations. Many others are more recent and some are only now beginning to assert themselves. It is important to observe these burgeonings. They may prove valuable in the furtherance of economy and lucidity and in making the language a yet finer instrument of communication. A few years ago *arbiter* and *arbitrator* were interchangeable. Today a valuable distinction is being made. An *arbiter* judges in his own right and is answerable to no one. A dress stylist, for example, is an arbiter of fashion. An *arbitrator* decides a particular issue referred to him by disputing parties. His decision is governed by law and he is responsible to codes of conduct and procedure outside himself. *Categorial* 'relating to or involving a category' is now usually distinguished from *categorical* 'unconditional, absolute'. *Indifference* signifies 'general apathy, lack of feeling for or against', whereas *indifferentism* means 'latitudinarianism and adiaphorism, especially in matters of religion'. An *informer* communicates information to the police: an *informant* supplies scientific data to a researcher. *Inquiry* means investigation and seeking after truth: an *enquiry* may be any question or request. *Instinctive* means 'determined by natural impulse or propensity': *instinctual* merely 'relating to instinct'. *Magistral* means 'masterly' in the sense of 'authoritative, superior, excellent': *magisterial* 'masterly' in the sense of 'authoritative, dictatorial'. *Normality* is 'the state of being normal, conformity with the norm': *normalcy* is limited to normality in economic, political, and social conditions, and so 'lack of tension'. *Racism* may be defined as 'the theory that certain races are superior to others': *racialism* signifies 'antagonism between races'. *Transcendent* means both 'non-immanent' and 'of supreme excellence': *transcendental* signifies 'visionary, idealistic, beyond experience'.

If the difference between two forms (e.g. *diplomat, diplomatist*) has failed to establish itself, or serves no valid purpose, it is rational and proper that one of the two should be dropped. On 5 January 1968 the diplomatic correspondent of *The Times* announced his intention to abandon *diplomatist*, recommended by H. W. Fowler in 1926, in favour of simpler *diplomat* (F *diplomate*).

MONOSYLLABISM

Side by side with this proliferation of polysyllabic compounds and derivatives we cannot fail to observe the opposite tendency to choose one-syllable words. In language, as in life, contrary tendencies may operate simultaneously, producing strength and beauty by juxtaposition. Even so, by such potent contrasts between sesquipedalians and monosyllables, Lady Macbeth answered her own question long ago:

> *Will all great Neptune's ocean wash this blood*
> *Clean from my hand? No, this my hand will rather*
> *The multitudinous seas incarnadine,*
> *Making the green one red.*
>
> *Macbeth* II ii 61

So, in 1947, modernized appearance in the latest Paris fashion suddenly became plain *new look*, and within a few days *new look* was a vogue phrase. It was not long before a chief executive became a *top man* and an intercontinental cable a *hot line*. A cookery book became plain *cookbook*.[1] British Railways suddenly

---

[1] Compare G *Kochbuch* (compound), F *cuisinière* (derivative) and Ital. *libro di cucina* (phrase).

appeared as *British Rail*. Noun attributives superseded gerunds
in numerous nominal phrases like *bank account* for banking
account, *lead singer* for leading singer, *spark plug* for sparking
plug, *swim suit* and *swim pool* for swimming costume and
swimming bath.

Clipped or stump words grew in fashion: *ad* (for advertisement), *crack* (wisecrack), *cyke* (cyclorama), *deb* (débutante),
fridge (refrigerator), *hood* (hoodlum), *jet* (jet-propelled
aircraft), *mike* (microphone), *op* (surgical operation), *quake*
(earthquake), *sax* (saxophone), and scores of others.

When, on 17 July 1841, Henry Mayhew launched *Punch*, and
not *Punchinello*, he anticipated the editors of later ages who
christened their journals *Drive, Flair, Flight, Fluke, Help, Life,
Look, Mind, Queen, She, Sun, Time, Which?, Where?, What?,
Wood* and *Word*. In 1964 the emigration of scientists to the
New World was labelled the *Brain Drain*. The Welfare State
claimed to nurse its citizens *from womb to tomb*, even when
financial deficits necessitated policies of *freeze* and *squeeze*.
Militant Negroes proclaimed *black power*, but hippies talked
about *flower power*, withdrawing from life's competitive
struggle or *rat race*. Mouth-to-mouth resuscitation of the
dying was called the *kiss of life*. Headliners wrote of *snap*
decisions, *key* industries, *crash* programmes, *end* products, and
good *buys*. Indeed, in banner headlines an adept or champion in
any capacity whatsoever now becomes an *ace*; even as any
aspiration, design, intention, object or purpose becomes an
aim; any denial, interdict, prohibition, refusal or restraint, a
ban; any attempt, endeavour, offer or tender, a *bid*; any
director, governor, leader, manager, overseer, ruler, superintendent or supervisor, a *chief*; any abbreviation, abridgement,
curtailment, diminution, reduction or shortening, a *cut*; any
adjustment, agreement, arrangement, bargain, concordat,
negotiation or transaction, a *deal*; any ceremony, exercise,
formal observance, procedure, ritual, routine or strict training,
a *drill*; any impetus, energetic action or organized effort, a
drive; any counterfeit, deception, false construction, fraud, hoax,
pretence, sham or simulation, a *fake*; any discrepancy, disparity,
hiatus or interval, a *gap*; any apprehension, foreboding,

foreknowledge, intuition, precognition or presentiment, a *hunch*; any achievement, employment, enterprise, occupation, performance, piece of work, profession, task or undertaking, a *job*; any assembly, conclave, conference, congregation, congress, convention or synod, a *meet*; any agreement, armistice, contract, covenant, engagement, pledge, protocol, stipulation, treaty or truce, a *pact*; any appeal, entreaty, petition, request or supplication, a *plea*; any exploration, inquiry, inquisition, investigation, research in depth, or scrutiny, a *probe*; any enquiry, examination by questioning, interrogatory or questionnaire, a *quiz*; any altercation, argument, brawl, brouhaha, conflict, contention, controversy, disagreement, discord, dispute, dissension, disturbance, fracas, quarrel, squabble or wrangle, a *row*; any calumny, defamation, denigration, depreciation, disparagement, libel, misrepresentation, slander or traducement, a *smear*; any accidental hitch, adventitious hindrance, sudden difficulty, unexpected obstacle or unforeseen impediment, a *snag*; any alternation, change over, exchange, interchange, reciprocation, transfer, transference or transposition, a *switch*; any address, allocution, conversation, discourse, harangue, lecture, monologue, oration or palaver, a *talk*; and any attempt, effort, endeavour, essay, experiment, proving, test, striving or trial, a *try*.

Lack of balance between exports and imports had long been known in America as the *dollar gap*. In the mid-sixties journalists began to use the expression *credibility gap* to indicate lack of balance between fact and fiction, and *image gap* to denote disparity between a person's actual character and his picture in the public eye. They lumped together all the differences in aims and attitudes between the old, the middle-aged and the young under the blanket term *intergenerational gap*.

An *in-thing* is something done by people (especially young people and avantgardists) who are 'in it'. *Admass*, first used by J. B. Priestley and Jacquetta Hawkes in *Journey down a Rainbow* (1955), is short for *ad*vertisement + *mass* media of communication. Through the universal media of press, radio and television *admass culture* is now accessible to all.

ALPHABETISMS AND ACRONYMS

If an initial-letter series, like CBE and FRS, is unpronounceable, we call it an *alphabetism*. If, like ANZAC and BANZARE, the series is pronounceable, we call it an *acronym*.

Abbreviations in writing and other forms of recorded speech are as old as language itself. They have always proved useful as time and space savers. To communicate efficiently, to make the other person understand perfectly, you need not 'tell all'. Abbreviations began with Sumerian, the first recorded language on earth. The Romans wrote AUC for *Anno urbis conditae*, counting time from the foundation of their city in the year 753 before the birth of Christ. They wrote SPQR for *Senatus populusque Romanus* 'Roman senate and people', therein expressing their democratic conception of the State. At the end of a friendly letter they put SVBEEV *Si vales, bene est, ego valeo* which might be loosely paraphrased 'I'm quite well, and I do so hope that you are too'.

In the modern world alphabetisms and acronyms proliferate abundantly, so much so that it is not easy to keep up with them. Their use is largely determined, not by any system, but by custom. No one, for instance, says [esp] for 'extra-sensory perception'. Everyone treats it as an alphabetism and says [i: es pi:]. No technician says HFDF for 'high frequency direction finder', a device for finding the direction of the source of a high-frequency radio valve. He says *huff-duff*. For 'sound radio and television' most people now say *radio and TV* without thinking. Telly, by the way, is now non-U. There is at present no sign that it will rise in status. The European Economic Community (or Common Market founded by the Treaty of Rome in 1957) is referred to as EEC and pronounced [i: i: si:] as an alphabetism, not [i:k] as an acronym. So, too, ICI or Imperial Chemical Industries is always referred to as [ai si: ai]. Most people say JP for Justice of the Peace in England, just as they say DA for District Attorney in America. But DJ for disc jockey is actually spelt *deejay* in America, just as a JC or member of the junior chamber (of commerce) is spelt *jaycee*, and a JV, or player for the junior varsity, is spelt *jayvee*. Custom alone decides that the Massachusetts Institute of Technology becomes, when abbreviated, *MIT* (an alphabetism) whereas its counterpart in California is designated *Cal Tech* (stump words). The editors of the monumental Goethe *Wörterbuch* (1945–2000) have deliberately specified that GWb shall be its title's only acceptable abbreviation.

However well known an alphabetism or acronym may be, courtesy demands that its full form should be spelt out at least once, preferably in the opening paragraph of any article or essay. After that the author is at liberty to use the recognized abbreviation as often as he pleases. This applies even to the most obvious acronyms like ASLIB (Association of Special Libraries and Information Bureaux), UCCA (Universities Central Council for Admissions), ESRO (European Space Research Organization), CARD (Campaign Against Racial Discrimination), NALGO (National Association of Local Government Officers) and UNICEF (United Nations International Children's Emergency Fund). As for lowercase acronyms like *eniac*, *ernie* and *auntie*, few people, when challenged, can rattle off without wavering 'electronic numerical integrator and computer', 'electronic random number indicator equipment', and 'automatic unit for national taxation and insurance'. Even the initial-letter origins of that neat quinquiliteral palindrome *radar* (radio detection and ranging) are not always readily recalled. Why should they be? There are now so many others: *maser* and *laser* (microwave and lightwave amplification by stimulated emission of radiation), *zeta* (zero energy thermonuclear apparatus), *dew* (distant early warning), *tiros* (television infra red observation satellite), and *mouse* (minimal orbital unmanned satellite of the earth). Many foreign acronyms have now acquired universal currency such as GUM, Moscow's State Store (Gosydarstvenniy Universalni Magazin); TASS, Russian news-gathering agency (Telegraphnoye Agenstvo SSSR), and its German counterpart DANA (Deutsche Allgemeine Nachrichten Agentur). The European Organization for Nuclear Research is always referred to by its French acronym CERN (Conseil européen de recherche nucléare).

BLENDS

Many hundreds of short words have arisen down the ages by blending or mixing echoic forms; some old, but others surprisingly recent. The process will doubtless continue.[1] *Echoic*, *imitative* or *onomatopoetic* words are those in which sound echoes sense. Think, for instance, of the noises made by the two noblest of animals, the horse and the dog. A horse neighs and a dog barks. But not only does a horse neigh; it snorts with anger and it whinnies with joy. Not only does a dog bark; it snaps, yaps, snarls, growls, whines and whimpers. 'This is the way the world ends', deplored T. S. Eliot in *The Hollow Men* –

> *This is the way the world ends*
> *Not with a bang but a whimper*

– and if you bang something with a crash (dash or smash) you bang-crash it, or bash it. *Bash* may be described as a blend of *bang* and *crash* etc., a two-into-one, telescoped word or blend. It may also be called a portmanteau word in accordance with Lewis Carroll's witty description of it in *Through the Looking Glass*:

> *O frabjous day! Callooh! Callay!*
> *He chortled in his joy.*

In other words, he chuckled like a hen and snorted like a horse. 'You see, it's like a portmanteau: there are two meanings packed up into one word.' Was Lewis Carroll, or Charles Lutwidge Dodgson (1832–98), aware that *churtle* had already been used for *chirp* or *chirrup* in Tudor English? He certainly had an uncanny insight into the mysterious subtleties of language. He helped to set that fashion in lighthearted wordplay which was later more fully exercised by James Joyce (1882–

---

[1] It is astonishing how many of the simplest words are of obscure origin. To explain the eight affixes of *incomprehensibility* added to its root *hen(d)*, or to describe the formation of *undiscoverably*, our longest word in which no letter occurs twice, is relatively easy. It is far more difficult to offer unimpeachable etymologies for common monosyllables like *big, boy, cut, fun, job, lad, lass, pull, put* and *jump*.

1941). People began to talk about *brunch* for breakfast and lunch in one meal; *drunch* for drinks plus lunch; and *dinter* for dinner combined with an interview. *Foggle* meant fog and drizzle; *smog*, smoke and fog; *smaze*, smoke and haze. *Motel* was the obvious portmanteau word for motorists' hotel, also called *autotel* or *autel*, later becoming *boatel* for a boat with hotel accommodation. In French, or rather *franglais* (itself a portmanteau word) *boatel* was adapted as *botatel*, with modified and respelt *bateau* substituted for *boat*. A *floatel* is a waterfront barge with hotel rooms. In Texas an airport hotel is an *airtel*. In California there are still, alas, sleazy suburbs or *slurbs*. London has its suburban utopia or *subtopia* and it has far too many *queuetopias* at its bus stops and supermarket checkouts. A procession of cabs may be described as a motorcar cavalcade or *motorcade*, undoubtedly American, whereas the lowly *moped*, or motorized pedal cycle, was first so named in West Germany. An oil that both lubricates and protects gives *lubritection*. A *travelogue* is a travel catalogue. A *cablegram* is a telegram sent by submarine cable. In cablese, by the way, a question mark becomes a *quark*, just as, in the realm of computers, a binary digit becomes a *bit*. In the best interests of compactness and brevity a moving staircase or escalading elevator has become an *escalator;* a non-vacuum electronic amplifier, or transfer resistor, has become a *transistor;* an amphibious tractor, an *amtrac;* a breath analyser, a *breathalyser*, and the condensation trail of jet aircraft, the *contrail*. In 1954 the European television network came into operation and was designated *Eurovision*. In 1968 the hovercraft port in Pegwell Bay was named *Hoverport*. The durable aluminium used in aircraft production is now called *duralumin*, and an alloy of magnesium and aluminium becomes *magnalium*. In the field of aeronautics a radar beacon becomes a *racon*, and in the domain of nuclear electronics or *nucleonics* a positive electron becomes a *positron*, whereas its negative opposite is designated a *negatron*. In the world of animal genetics the offspring of a male tiger and a lioness is a *tigon*: that of a lion and a tigress is a *liger*. In the nomenclature of astrophysics a distant quasi stellar source of radio energy is now called a *quasar*.

BACKFORMATION

Backformation may be defined as regressive or negative derivation, or derivation in reverse. New words are created by analogy from existing words that are assumed to be derivatives. Thus the verb *edit* is made from the agent noun *editor* on the reversed analogy of *actor* from *to act*. Although logically irregular, since it is based upon false assumptions, backformation is not psychologically irrational. The Indian raja who addressed a British official as 'Most becile sir!' backformed his epithet rationally on the ground that every negative adjective has a positive counterpart. 'Do you kipple?' was an Edwardian pleasantry meaning 'Are you an admiring reader of Rudyard Kipling?' 'Orthodoxy,' whispered Bishop William Warburton wantonly, 'is my doxy: heterodoxy is another man's doxy.' In so punning, he was actually bestowing another homonym upon the language. Theologians now use *doxy* as a synonym for 'mode of belief', much as laymen speak of *isms* and *ologies*. Backformations may sound frivolous in conversation and they may look slightly suspect in print – verbs like *enthuse, liaise* and *reminisce*, reversely derived from the nouns *enthusiasm, liaison* and *reminiscence*. Nevertheless some backformations are serious and important. For instance, the noun *greed* from *greedy*, the adjective *difficult* from *difficulty*, and the verb *grovel* from *grovelling*. The following table is confined to verbs backformed from nouns and adjectives. Dates of earliest recordings before 1933 are taken from the OED and its First Supplement. After that year they are only approximate:

Verb	*Backformed from*	*First known instance*
beg	Beghard	1225
suckle	suckling	1408
cobble	cobbler	1496
hawk	hawker	1542
partake	part taker	1561
laze	lazy	1592
grovel	grovelling	1593
eavesdrop	eavesdropper	1606

locate	location	1652
edit	editor	1791
donate	donation	1795
process	procession	1814
reminisce	reminiscence	1829
loaf	loafer	1838
intuit	intuition	1840
housekeep	housekeeper	1842
donate	donation	1845
orate	oration	1858
enthuse	enthusiasm	1859
diagnose	diagnosis	1861
burgle	burglar	1870
electrocute	electrocution	1889
commute	commuter	1890
liaise	liaison	1915
peeve	peevish	1918
sculpt	sculptor	1934
frivol	frivolous	1940
bulldoze	bulldozer	1941
automate	automation	1950
televise	television	1950
escalate	escalation	1955
sightsee	sightseeing	1960

A Beghard was a member of a mendicant brotherhood modelled on the Beguines. Eaves 'roof edge' comes from OE *efes*, but MHG *obese* (G dialect *obsen*), like its Gothic cognate *ubizwa*, meant also a porch. An eavesdropper is one who stands under the overhanging roof (or in the porch) and listens to private conversation going on within. The verb commute meaning 'to exchange, interchange' comes straight from Lat. *com-mutare* (1633), but in the sense 'to travel between home and work' it is clearly an independent backformation. A New Yorker named Diebold reduced automaticization (G *Automatizierung, Selbststeuerung* 'machines operated by remote control') to *automation* in 1952. The verb *frivol* was perhaps first used by Dorothy

Sayers (1893–1957): 'A man of weight . . . does not come and frivol in the typists' room' (quoted in Webster III 1961).

Although blending and backforming must be regarded as irregular morphological processes, they are very much alive today. They play no small part both in everyday speech and in that new vocabulary of science to which we must now direct our attention.

CHAPTER 4

Scientific Vocabulary

IT IS axiomatic that a new thing, whether discovered or invented, if it is unlike any other thing already known to man, requires a new word to identify it. If the new thing has international status, the new term will quickly become universal in the modern world where communication is nearly instantaneous.

NEO-HELLENIC COMPONENTS

In the ever expanding world of science and invention most of these new words are either taken direct from Greek or compounded of Greek elements. This applies not only to English but also to the other three widely disseminated languages – French, Spanish and Portuguese. Moreover, and in some ways more important still, this also applies to Russian. The modified Cyrillic 33-letter alphabet of modern Russian is based upon the 22-letter alphabet of Greek which is the same today as it was in the time of Plato and Aristotle. Ties between Kiev, Byzantium and Athens have been close throughout the ages.

It is indeed most fortunate that the scientists of the two leading powers – the United States and the Soviet Union – both go to Greek for their technical terms. Scientists now have at their disposal a copious store of neo-Hellenic components. They have come to regard the Greek language as a kind of quarry from which they can mine blocks to be shaped at need to make new words or to adapt forms already in use. For instance, by prefixing the adverb *tele* 'distant' to the existing compound *photography* they make the unambiguous term *telephotography* to denote the photographing of remote objects by means of a special lens. Again, by inserting the adjective *micro-* 'small' into this same compound they create the term *photomicrography* to denote the photographing of minute organisms like bacteria and viruses which are quite invisible to the naked eye. As areas of investigation are subdivided, so fresh word blocks are excavated from this rich neo-Hellenic quarry to supply labels for the new specialisms. As the old life sciences of botany and zoology are further departmentalized, so new names arise like *cytology* (study of cell structure), *dendrology* (trees), *ecology* (environment), *mycology* (fungi), *pedology* (science of soils), *phytogenesis* (plant evolution); *embryology* (antenatal foetus), *entomology* (insects), *herpetology* (reptiles and amphibians), *ichthyology* (fish), *ornithology* (birds), *paleontology* (fossils), *zoogeography* (animal distribution), and many more. All these names are, you will observe, neo-Hellenic, whereas the names of the older applied sciences are Latin: *agriculture* (field crops and animal husbandry), *silviculture* (forestry) and *horticulture* (cultivation of garden plants).

BOTANY AND ZOOLOGY

You might argue, of course, that the binary nomenclature of plants established so securely by Carl von Linné (1707–78), alias Carolus Linnaeus, Professor of Botany in the University of Uppsala, is just pure Latin and therefore does not properly belong to the vocabulary of English. Many names, it is true, go back to Pliny the Elder (Gaius Plinus Secundus, AD 23–79) who wrote his rambling *Naturalis Historia* in thirty-seven books before being choked in the prime of life by the fumes from the suddenly re-erupting Mount Vesuvius. Linné owed much to Pliny and more still to his immediate predecessors, some of whom he met in his extensive study journeys in England, France and Holland. He and they took Latin for granted. Linné was a true son of the eighteenth century in that he loved order above all things. 'His love of order was greater than his love of nature.' In 1753, just two years before the appearance of Johnson's Dictionary, he published his *Species Plantarum*, in which he introduced the so-called binomial system of two terms denoting genus and species, in place of a descriptive phrase. For instance, instead of calling the common buttercup *ranunculus foliis serratis, scapo nudo unifloro* he labelled it *Ranunculus bulbosus* and that has been its universal name ever since.[1] To us it remains the buttercup, even as to Germans it is still *Butterblume* 'butter flower' and to the French *bouton d'or* 'gold bud or button'. The daisy, that meadow flower so loved by Chaucer and Burns, had appeared as plain *bellis* in Pliny, but was designated *Bellis perennis* in Linné's binomial taxonomy. To Germans it is *Gänseblümchen* 'little goose flower' and to the French *pâquerette* 'little paschal (flower)'. To us, as to Chaucer, it is 'day's eye', opening its petals slowly with the rising sun and closing them again at eventide.

> *The longe day I shoop me for t'abide*
> *For nothing elles, and I shal nat lye,*
> *But for to loke upon the dayesie*
> *That wel by reson men it calle may*
> *The dayesye or elles the ye of day,*
> *The emperice and flour of floures alle.*[2]

Do you say *delphinium* or *larkspur, antirrhinum* or *snapdragon, belladonna* or *deadly nightshade*? You are here concerned with two languages, and it is good to know them both. You are really concerned with two languages when you visit the Botanical Gardens at Kew or elsewhere: *Populus tremula* or *aspen, Salix babylonica* or *weeping willow, Taxodium distichum* or *swamp cypress, Lonicera periclymenum* or *honeysuckle*.

Do you say *feline* or *catlike?* Numerous adjectives in *-ine* – *asinine* (pertaining to asses), *bovine* (oxen), *canine* (dogs), *equine* (horses), *hircine* (goats), *leporine* (hares), *lupine* (wolves), *ovine* (sheep), *phocine* (seals), *vulpine* (foxes);

---

[1] The name of the genus, normally capitalized, is a noun in the nominative singular. That of the species may be another noun in apposition, a noun in the genitive singular or plural, an adjective or a present participle. Genera are grouped into families, families into orders, orders into classes, classes into phyla, and phyla into three kingdoms: animal, vegetable and mineral.

[2] Geoffrey Chaucer, *The Legend of Good Women*, Text F, 180–85.

accipitrine (hawks), *anserine* (geese), *aquiline* (eagles), *corvine* (crows), *passerine* (perchers and sparrows), *psittacine* (parrots); and *lacertine* (lizards) – remind us that zoology, like botany, has drawn upon traditional Latin for its basic nomenclature. Since the eighteenth century, however, zoology and botany have followed medicine and chemistry in going more and more to Greek for the names of specialized concepts.

MEDICINE AND CHEMISTRY

The so-called *Hippocratic Corpus* was put together in Greek-speaking Alexandria in the third century before Christ and that 'prince of physicians' Claudius Galen (AD 130–200) wrote his pioneering medical treatises in Greek. Through Arabic translations Galen dominated medical teaching in the Dark and Middle Ages. When the original texts became available again to the western world in the early sixteenth century, Greek was being taught for the first time at both Oxford and Cambridge. As the language of medicine, Greek has behind it a tradition of over two thousand years. As the language of chemistry, it has behind it a tradition of only two centuries. Modern chemistry had its beginnings in the eighteenth century when that distinguished French scientist, Antoine Laurent Lavoisier (1743–94), deliberately chose Greek for his technical terms. That choice was indeed decisive. Lavoisier did for chemistry what Newton did for physics. He showed that the air was a mixture of *oxygène* 'acidifying element' or 'acid producing' and *azote* 'not life-supporting', later renamed *nitrogène* 'nitre producing'. Water, he demonstrated later, was a compound of *oxygène* and *hydrogène*. In 1787, collaborating with other members of the *Académie des Sciences*, Lavoisier compiled his epoch-making *Méthode de nomenclature chimique*.

French was still the first language of Europe and western chemists naturally followed Lavoisier in this matter of nomenclature with the important exception of the Germans who were already obsessed by the notion of linguistic purity or *reines deutsch*. The Germans therefore named oxygen, hydrogen and nitrogen *Sauerstoff* 'sour stuff', *Wasserstoff* 'water stuff' and *Stickstoff* 'choke stuff', and, in so doing, they cut themselves off from the rest of the scientific world. Moreover, they made other needless difficulties for themselves. As new fields of research opened out from the older sciences, it became increasingly hard, if not impossible, for them to find native names that were both precise and comprehensible. Today the clash persists. German scientists must now choose between *Fruchtkeimwissenschaft* and *Embryologie, Altertumskunde* and *Archäologie,* and so on. Little by little, however, they are being forced by necessity to abandon cumbersome native compounds and derivatives and to adopt the neo-Hellenic terminology of their neighbours. In Russia there has been no such clash. Soviet scientists are genuinely pragmatic. They have no such inhibiting qualms about linguistic purity. In any case, recognizing that the modified Cyrillic script of modern Russian is not far removed from that of both ancient and modern Athens, they feel themselves at home with new Greek words. When, on 12 April 1961, Yuri A. Gagarin was orbited round the earth in under two hours in the six-ton satellite Vostok, he was immediately hailed as the world's first *cosmonaut.* This brand-new Greek compound became an international word overnight because, thanks to instantaneous telecommunication, the whole world shared in the glad news of this latest achievement in man's conquest of space.

ISV

The alphabetism ISV, International Scientific Vocabulary, was invented by Dr Charles Sleeth of Princeton University when he compiled etymologies for Webster III of 1961. As stated in the Explanatory Notes (§ 7. 6, p.18a):

A considerable part of the technical vocabulary of the sciences and other specialized studies consists of words or word elements that are current in two or more languages with only such slight modifications as are necessary to adapt them to the structure of the individual language in each case. Many words and word elements of this kind have become sufficiently a part of the general vocabulary of English to require entry in a general dictionary of our language. On account of the vast extent of the relevant published material in many languages and in many scientific and other specialized fields, it is impracticable to ascertain the language of origin of every such term, yet it would not be accurate to formulate a statement about the origin of any such term in a way that could be interpreted as implying that it was coined in English. Accordingly, wherever a term that is entered in this dictionary belongs recognizably to this class of internationally current terms, and no positive evidence is at hand to show that it was coined in English, the etymology recognizes its international status and the possibility that it originated elsewhere than in English by use of the label ISV (for International Scientific Vocabulary).

When he refers to many scientific terms that have become 'a part of the general vocabulary' Dr Sleeth puts his finger on one of the main problems now confronting all lexicographers. The editors of *The Oxford Dictionary* felt justified in excluding many thousands of technical words from their work on the ground that these had already received adequate treatment in the highly specialized glossaries of the sciences concerned. To what extent is this principle still valid? Many neologisms created yesterday by specialists are today heard in general conversation. They have moved in from the lexical periphery towards the common centre. In his decision to accept or reject them the lexicographer has no longer any sure and infallible criterion. His final choice remains an arbitrary one more than ever before.

The nomenclature of genetics, for example, has been created almost entirely in the present century. *Gamete* 'reproductive cell, whether sperm or egg' (Gk *gametē* 'wife', *gamétēs* 'husband'), it is true, was first used in 1886 and *zygote* 'cell produced by the union of two gametes' (Gk *zygōtós* 'yoked') in 1891. *Chromosome* 'colour body' appeared about the same time and *genetics* itself was first defined as 'the experimental study of heredity and variation' by the sociologist Lester Frank Ward of Columbia University in 1897. *Gene*, a variant of *gen*, made its earliest appearance in 1913 in the seventh edition of Dorland's *Illustrated Medical Dictionary*. In the spring of 1953 a major breakthrough was made by Francis Crick and James Watson in their initiation of *molecular biology* as a special branch of genetics and in their pioneering investigations of the chemical and physical properties of that essential constituent of all chromosomes and genes known as DNA or deoxyribonucleic acid.

Chaucer referred to 'fermacies of herbes' in *The Knight's Tale* (1386) and Nathan Bailey defined pharmacology in his *Universal Etymological English Dictionary* of 1721 as 'a Treatise concerning the Art of preparing Medicines'. Pharmacology is, in fact, 'the science or theory of pharmacy' and here we should do well to observe the more recent development of *psychopharmacology* or the study of the psychological effects of drugs on human beings. It became a useful blanket term in the 1950s when more and more people, especially young people, were experimenting with psychodelic or mind-dilating opiates like *cannabis* (Gk *kánnabis* cognate with OE *hænep* 'hemp'), *heroin* (trade name cynically associated with Gk *hḗrōs* 'hero'), *psilocybin* (Gk *psilo(s)* 'bare' + *kýbē* 'head', *psilocybe* being a kind of mushroom + suffix *-in*) and LSD or lysergic acid diethylamide.

Auguste Comte invented the term *sociologie* in his *Cours de Philosophie Positive* (1830–42) and in 1843 this term made its first appearance as *sociology* in English.[1] Because it was a hybrid deriving its first component from Latin and its second from Greek, the new term was scorned by purists.[2] Nevertheless, it was used without apology by Herbert Spencer in his extensive treatise on *Principles of Sociology* (1876–96) and by Lester Frank Ward in his *Dynamic Sociology* (1883) and *Pure Sociology* (1903). Today sociology is a fully established discipline closely linked with anthropology, demography, economics and ethnology.

[1] 'These are to constitute a new science, to be called Social Ethics, or Sociology'. Blackwood's Magazine LIII 397. See OED s.v. *sociology* 'the science or study of the origin, history, and constitution of human society; social science'.

[2] 'The new science of sociology, as it is barbarously termed.' *Fraser's Magazine* XLIV (1851) 452.

LINGUISTIC HYBRIDS

In this new world of ISV referential precision is surely more important than linguistic purity. When, for instance, R. A. Zsigmondy invented in 1903 a dark-field compound microscope for the detection and scrutiny of objects too small to be seen through the finest existing microscope, he named it an *ultramicroscope*. He could not, in fact, have done better. If, on the ground of linguistic purism, he had insisted on using the Greek prepositional prefix *hyper-*, and called his invention a *hypermicroscope*, he would have given it a misleading label. As a living prefix *hyper-* denotes 'over, above, exceeding, excessive'. It does not signify 'over, above, beyond' like Lat. *ultra*, in the direction of diminution. Classical constituents, it is important to observe, are now acquiring new and precise meanings in the best interests of scientific accuracy. Obviously, then, their ulterior etymologies and their significations in classical antiquity no longer entirely determine present usage. Gk *hyper* and Lat. *super* are cognate with E *over*, but whereas *hypersonic* refers to speeds five or more times greater than that of sound in the same medium, *supersonic* denotes any speed higher than that of sound. A supersonic plane is one capable of achieving such speed. Supersonics is that branch of science which is concerned with supersonic phenomena. *Ultrasonic*, however, is a term limited to the field of acoustics. It is applied to sound waves of such pitch as to be beyond (or beneath) the threshold of human audibility.

When, in 1926, John Logie Baird, an electrical engineer trained at the Glasgow Royal Technical College, demonstrated television in Soho, he deliberately chose that hybrid appellation in preference to such pure Greek compounds as *telopsis* or *telorama*. His choice was, by general consent, a good one.[1]

When, on 10 July 1962, United States engineers launched the medium-altitude television satellite at Cape Canaveral, they

[1] The adverb *tēle* functioned as an adjectival prefix even in Classical Greek in forms like *tēlaugés* (with *-e* dropped before a vowel) 'far-shining, conspicuous' and *tēleskópos* 'far-seeing' (whence our *telescope*), but its Latin synonym *procul* was never so used. *Proculvision* would therefore have been both cacophonous and unprecedented.

christened it *Telstar*, not *Telaster*. This, too, was appropriate since this two-syllable hybrid, pronounced with level stress, was a portmanteau formation from *television star*. It was an impressive name for the first manmade satellite linking televised broadcasts between Andover, Maine, and European stations in Cornwall and Brittany.

In synonymous derivatives like *peripatetic* and *circumambulatory*, *periphery* and *circumference*, *periphrasis* and *circumlocution*, the Greek and Latin prefixes have identical meanings, but in the realm of medicine they show slight divergences. *Peri-* has acquired the nuance of enclosing or encasing. For instance, the *pericardium* is the membranous sac enclosing the heart. *Perivisceral* implies enclosing the intestines and not merely surrounding them. It would be pointless and unprofitable to rewrite this hybrid as all-Latin *circumvisceral* on the one hand or as all-Greek *periplanchnic* on the other.[1] Nevertheless one sympathizes with those chemists who insist on *univalent*, *bivalent*, *quadrivalent* and *quinquivalent* instead of traditional *monovalent*, *divalent*, *tetravalent* and *pentavalent*.[2] In the younger science of genetics *univalent* and *bivalent*, as applied to chromosomes, are the only accepted forms. It is interesting to note that *kilo-*, formed arbitrarily from Gk *khílioi* 'thousand' indicates multiplication in *kilometre*, whereas *milli-*, combining form of Lat. *mille* 'thousand' denotes division in *millimetre*. In the 1950s, in order to meet the need for infinitesimal measurements, especially in molecular biology, the prefix *nano-*, combining form of Gk *nânos* 'dwarf' was adopted, as in *nanometre* 'one millionth part of a millimetre'.

LINGUISTIC MALFORMATIONS

It was exceedingly odd that Sigmund Freud (1856–1939), who had read Greek at school, should have talked about *Psychoanalyse*, and not *Psychanalyse*, in a paper published in 1896

[1] So T. H. Savory, *The Language of Science*, London, Deutsch 1967, p. 69.

[2] No question arises with *trivalent* since *tri-* is the combining form of both Gk *treis*, *tria* and Lat. *trēs*, *tria*.

expounding his doctrine of the philosophy of the unconscious or *die Philosophie des Unbewussten*. Greek linking -o- in compounds regularly falls out before vowels and anyone possessing *Sprachgefühl* for the noblest language ever spoken by man cannot fail to deplore its intrusion into this cacophonous neologism. The French would not hear of it. Tetrasyllabic *psychanalyse* [psikanaliz] has ever been the only accepted form in that language. The French Academy saw to that. It was all the more unfortunate that J. J. Putnam imported 'psycho-analysis' into an essay contributed to the *Journal of Abnormal Psychology* in 1906 and that British and American psychologists have since followed him like sheep.[1]

It was no less odd that the jocular term *psychedelic* (coined by medical students at Harvard University in 1961 as a playful combination of Gk *psȳchē* 'soul' and *dēl(os)* 'visible, evident' + *ic*) should have been adopted (without proper revision to *psychodelic*) by the whole western world. It quickly caught on as an *in-word* among *with-it, switched-on, trendy* devotees of the 'consciousness-expanding cult'. In the twilight realms of hallucinogenic flower power its derivative *psychedelia* became a near-synonym of *euphoria*, that inner feeling of 'well-bearing' or 'well-being' which has little or no relation with the realities of the outer world.

POPULARIZED TECHNICALITIES

Under the influence of radio, television and the quality press we are witnessing a remarkable breaking down of barriers between scientific and popular vocabularies. People talk of *pediatrics* instead of *child care*. The terms are, of course, synonymous; but by no means interchangeable in every situational context. *Pediatrics* is neo-Hellenic, technical, clinical, medical, pro-

[1] Murray, who spent five years (1904–09) editing P- words for OED, was justified in ignoring Putnam's recent importation, but Onions admitted it without comment into the 1933 Supplement. It appeared as solid *psychoanalysis* in Webster II of 1934 and in the third edition of SOED in 1944. In Webster III of 1961 and in RHD of 1966 it was printed solid together with *psychanalysis* as the corrected alternative.

fessional: *child care* is Anglo-Saxon, familiar, warm-hearted, intimate, human. People also talk of *geriatrics* when they mean care of old folk. They even use the highly abstract term *gerontology* signifying the scientific study of the phenomena of aging. It is strange that we English have no one word for 'old person' corresponding to Gk *gérōn*, Lat. *senex*, F *vieillard* and G *Greis*. From the root *sen* of Lat. *senex* come the derivatives *senile*, *senility* and *senescence*. Whereas, earlier in this century people would say that someone was suffering from consumption (by which they meant phthisis or pulmonary consumption) they now say *tuberculosis* or *TB*. They now talk of a *coronary thrombosis*, or plain *coronary*, instead of a heart attack; *poliomyelitis*, or *polio*, instead of infantile paralysis; and *laryngitis* instead of sore throat. A throat specialist now calls himself a *laryngologist* or, yet more portentously, an *otorhinolaryngologist*, since, inevitably, he must examine ears and nose as well. Whereas before people had sore eyes, they now suffer from *conjunctivitis*. They no longer have a gum boil, but *ulcerous gingivitis*. If they have an itching skin, they suffer from some form of *dermatitis*. Gout is now *rheumatoid arthritis*, and its victim is said to be *arthritic*. Feeling run down, he is told that he is suffering from nervous exhaustion or *neurasthenia*. If he finds himself hating the very sight of food, he is consoled by having his condition diagnosed as *anorexia*. If he has a fit of the blues, or is down in the dumps, he is now said to be the victim of *manic-depressive psychosis;* and if he has an uneven temperament 'now up, now down, like bucket in a well', now exuberant and ebullient and now doleful and despondent, his is merely an interesting case of *cyclothymia*. Compelled, after an accident, to spend a freezing cold night on the mountains, he is found to be suffering, not from exposure, but from *hypothermia*. In junky language a drug addict is sick, straight or high. If high, he enjoys *euphoria* or *psychedelia*, as already mentioned. Hardening of the arteries, that ineluctable concomitant of old age well known to Galen, sounds not quite so bad when we call it *arteriosclerosis*.

Was Wystan Hugh Auden justified in labelling our time an Age of Anxiety? It is truly astonishing how many phobias or morbid fears afflict contemporary society, but let us not take them too seriously! Here are just a few: *agoraphobia* (abnormal dread of open spaces), *ailurophobia* (morbid fear of cats), *anthropophobia* (people in general), *bathophobia* (depths), *carcinophobia* (cancer), *claustrophobia* (closed places), *cremnophobia* (overhanging cliffs), *cynophobia* (dogs), *dysmorphophobia* (physical deformity), *entomophobia* (insects), *ergophobia* (work), *gerontophobia* (old age), *hydrophobia* (morbid fear of water; rabies as a specific disease in man), *hypsophobia* (heights), *monophobia* (being alone), *necrophobia* (dead bodies), *ornithophobia* (birds), *pedophobia* (children), *photophobia* (light), *psychophobia* (psychiatric treatment), *pyrophobia* (fire), *scopophobia* (being seen), *scotophobia* (darkness), *thanatophobia* (death), *topophobia* (certain places), *xenophobia* (foreigners), not to forget *triskaidekaphobia* (suspicious fear of the number thirteen). You will probably have no difficulty in adding to this list. As you see, they are all good neo-Hellenic creations except *agoraphobia*, irregular for *agorophobia*, and its antonym *claustrophobia* which, as a quite unnecessary Latin-Greek hybrid, is readily modifiable to all-Greek *cleistrophobia*.

It is interesting to recall that as long ago as 1839 William Henry Fox Talbot read a paper to the Royal Society – he had been elected a Fellow at the early age of twenty-two – entitled 'Some account of the Art of Photogenic Drawing, or the Process by which Natural Objects may be made to delineate themselves without the aid of the Artist's Pencil'. By 'Photogenic Drawing' Talbot meant *photography*, a term first recorded a few months later in a paper read to the same society by Sir John Herschel. Today *photogenic* is still used in special senses in biology and medicine. Since 1960, however, it has come into popular use again. It is applied to persons and objects who form an attractive subject for photography and look well in a photograph. A sitter for a portrait may be said to have photogenic hands. Similarly people or things possessing physical qualities or characteristics that televise well are said to be *telegenic* or *videogenic*. They are said to be *radiogenic* if they broadcast well on sound radio, but we should not forget that this adjective remains in use as a technical term in physics meaning 'produced

D

by radioactive decay or radioactivity'. Lytton Strachey, someone tells us, was *allergic* to the telephone: he just didn't like using it. When we read of a popular model's *vital statistics* (bust, waist, and hip measurements) we do not cease to be aware of the demographical signification of this expression (births, marriages and deaths). How many people really regard *ergonomics* (or *biotechnology*) as a serious academic discipline? It is 'human engineering', concerned with problems relating to mutual adjustments between men and machines. Because the Athenians used pebble-stones in casting votes, someone has invented *psephology* as the technical term to denote the study of elections and electioneering. Meddling officials are now said to suffer from an *interferiority complex*. Theodore Besterman has just coined *autobibliographer* to indicate an author who has taken the trouble to compile a bibliography of his own published writings.

PRECISION AND IMPRECISION

Some people like to be different and they think they are impressing their hearers, if not scoring a point, when they say *ambience* instead of environment or surroundings, *mentality* instead of mind or disposition; *authentic* for true, *idiosyncratic* for peculiar, *vulnerable* for weak, and *viable* for workable. A seed is viable if it is capable of germination. How can a plan or an enterprise be viable, even in a transferred sense? But *viable* sounds well. That is the important thing. Used thus loosely, however, its meaning ceases to be sharp and clear. Its edges are blunted. Long ago *hectic* and *chronic* suffered from this kind of loose usage. Hectic fever was the habitual distemper accompanying phthisis or dysentery: only in colloquial speech and slang did *hectic* come to mean 'exciting, wild, impassioned'. A chronic disease was one lasting a long time, or apt to recur: only in colloquial speech or slang did *chronic* come to mean 'bad, intense, severe'. An *alibi* is not any excuse or reason (with a suggestion of dishonesty or evasiveness) but an accused person's legal defence that he was *al-ibi* or *else-where* at the time of the crime. *Ambivalence* is not the same as ambiguity: it rather implies something akin to 'mixed feelings'. It is a psychological term denoting the co-existence in one person of contradictory emotional attitudes like love and hate, or reverence and contempt, for the same object. *Arguable* does not mean the same as disputable, uncertain, open to question. A logical proposition is said to be arguable if it has sufficient probability to be capable of support by argument. *Dichotomy* does not mean the same as bipartition. In logic it signifies classification by separation into two mutually exclusive and exhaustive divisions. A *dilemma* is something more subtle than a simple choice of alternatives. In logic it is a syllogism in which the major premiss consists of two assumptions and the minor premiss is an exhaustive disjunctive proposition. (If A, then B; if C, then D. Either A or C. Therefore, either B or D.) *Extrapolation* is not merely conjectural extension into the future based upon knowledge of the past. In mathematics it is the statistical calculation of the value of a variable outside (Lat. *extra*) its tabulated or observed range. *Miscegenation* does not contain the prefix *mis-* but the component *misce-* from Lat. *miscēre* 'to mix'. It signifies 'mixed breeding', neither more nor less, without subaudition of right or wrong.[1] *Nostalgia* comes from Gk *nóstos* 'homecoming' and *álgos* 'pain' by way of neo-Latin *nostalgia* translating G *Heimweh* 'home woe'. It means 'homesickness, deep and persistent longing for home'. But again, it sounds well. It is applied (or misapplied) by novelists to any sentimental yearning or vague longing, especially for things of the past.[2] A *phenomenon* (first used by Francis Bacon in *The Advancement of Learning* in 1605) is not necessarily an extraordinary or remarkable person or thing, but any appearance or object perceived. In Kantian philosophy it is a thing that appears to the mind from without as distinguished from a

---

[1] Etymologically it is a malformation, compounded irregularly from Lat. *miscere* 'to mix' + *genus* 'race' + E suffix *-ation*. According to ODEE, it was 'said to have been copyrighted in 1863 by D. G. Croly of New York'.

[2] 'The terror, the agony, the nostalgia of the heathen past was a constant torture to her mediumistic soul.' D. H. Lawrence, *The Lost Girl*, Chapter 15.

noumenon that appears to the mind from within and is therefore an object of purely intellectual intuition. We could go on extending this list indefinitely.

Is any harm done by such loose uses of language? None at all, if careful speakers and writers persist resolutely in bending words back to their strict senses whenever they themselves use them in serious discourse, and if lexicographers distinguish accurately between scientific and popular senses and show, with adequate illustrations, when and how words are used strictly, loosely, scientifically, colloquially, in slang and in vulgar parlance. The more we come to think of it, the more we realize how important dictionaries are. Looking ahead, we see that the great dictionaries of tomorrow will inevitably acquire greater and greater authority and power. We see, too, that the scientific world language of the future will not be made by any one nation. It will emerge as a medium of communication created by common sense, practical convenience and growing necessity. In its present stage it appears to be almost entirely limited to names of substances and processes. That is true, but, next to verbs, nouns do in fact constitute the most important word-class or part of speech. Changes in the functions of nouns and nominal phrases will claim our attention in the following chapter.

CHAPTER 5

Nouns and Nominal Groups

OUR WESTERN civilization, it has been said, favours an over-development of the intellect at the expense of the emotions. That is why people prefer nouns to verbs. They suffer from what the Germans call *Substantivseuche* 'noun disease'. Instead of saying quite simply and straightforwardly 'London is growing rapidly', they say 'London's growth is rapid'. And they say 'John's arrival was premature' instead of 'John came too soon'.

'London's growth is rapid' is a simple sentence consisting of subject (noun premodified by another noun in the genitive case) + copula (mere link-verb with no inherent meaning of its own, being a mere marker of predication, and therefore omitted in many languages) + predicative adjective as complement. We call *growth* an abstract noun because it refers to the action or state of *growing* as something 'drawn away' (Lat. *abs-tractus*) from concrete reality.

'London is growing rapidly' is a simple sentence consisting of a subject (proper noun) + verbal group (present progressive tense, third person singular) + adverb of manner modifying the action named by the verb.

PREDOMINANCE OF NOUNS OVER VERBS

The above sentences mean the same, but the viewpoints are slightly different.

'John's arrival was premature' is a simple sentence consisting of subject (noun premodified by another noun in the genitive case) + simple past tense of the verb *to be* (not a meaningless copula here because it refers to past time and it is therefore expressed in most languages) + predicative adjective as complement. We do not label *arrival* an abstract noun because it is the equivalent of the gerund *arriving*, merely naming (without abstracting) the action of the verb.

'John came too soon' is a simple sentence consisting of proper noun (the commonest of all European forenames used conventionally by linguists in their illustrative sentences to denote a particular male person instead of an unrelated *he* of uncertain reference) + intransitive verb in the simple past tense + intensive adverb of degree modifying a following adverb of time.

Again, the two sentences mean the same, but the viewpoints are slightly different. *John's arrival*, a nominal group, endocentric, has the head word *arrival* which names the action of coming to a particular place and focuses the hearer's attention upon John's sudden appearance. *John came*, subject-predicate construction, exocentric, simply states the action of coming at some point in past time. But there are further differences in lexis or vocabulary. The Romance words *arrival* and *premature*, meaning ultimately 'coming to land' and 'ripened before (due time)' are here obviously used metaphorically. They contrast impressively with the Anglo-Saxon monosyllables *came too soon*.

In each of the following pairs of sentences the first is characteristic of that current form of expression which shows a preponderance of nouns over verbs, whereas the second is briefer and more direct:

A cessation of work on the cathedral fabric will take place throughout August
　　Cathedral repairs will be suspended during August
The old man's search for alternative accommodation met with no success
　　The old man could find nowhere else to live
Participation by the workers in factory management is absolutely non-existent
　　The workers have no say at all in the running of their factory
Early expectation of a vacancy is indicated by the manager
　　The manager expects to be able to announce a vacancy soon

Is there any evidence of this applicant's excessive road accident proneness?

Can you show that this applicant (for a car insurance policy) is more likely to be involved in accidents than others?

Practical effectiveness requires disregard of personal credit

The way to get things done is not to mind who gets the credit for doing them

A wide age differentiation is discernible among the candidates applying for this post

Candidates for this post are of very different ages

Your disablement pension entitlement is now satisfactorily placed beyond all dispute on legal grounds

As a disabled person you are legally entitled to a pension

Notice carefully the composition of that initial nominal group in the first sentence of that last pair. It consists of the head word *entitlement* preceded by the two adjunct nouns *disablement pension* which themselves constitute an independent nominal group when detached. It is (as we shall be seeing later in this chapter) a type far too common in present-day officialese. It is, indeed, a structure quite peculiar to English among the great languages of the world.

You may amuse yourself sampling texts along the lines suggested by the above pairs of sentences. You can indeed do this fairly quickly by taking the opening paragraphs of, say, the classical novels of the eighteenth century and comparing them with any recent novels you may happen to have read. You will probably find plenty of evidence to support my present thesis – the predominance of nouns over verbs in the modern world.

Julius Caesar was a man of action. In jocular mood, you might prove that he was the man of action *par excellence* because he alone, in all human history, spoke an all-verb sentence of three words.[1]

[1] *Veni, vidi, vici* 'I came, I saw, I conquered'. Caesar actually recorded these words in a message to Rome announcing his victory at Zela in 47 B.C.

Compare the opening sentence of *The Pilgrim's Progress* (1678) –

As I walked through the wilderness of this world, I lighted on a certain place where was a Den, and I laid me down in that place to sleep: and, as I slept, I dreamed a dream

– with the first two sentences of Aldous Huxley's *Brave New World* (1932) –

A squat grey building of only thirty-four storeys. Over the main entrance the words CENTRAL LONDON HATCHERY AND CONDITIONING CENTRE, and, in a shield, the World State's motto, COMMUNITY, IDENTITY, STABILITY.

Both texts introduce visions in vivid contrast: the one biblical and celestial, the other scientific and terrestrial.

John Bunyan uses six finite verbs, one infinitive of purpose, six nouns and one adjective (not counting determiners).

Dispensing with verbs altogether, Aldous Huxley uses eleven nouns as head words, four attributive adjectives (not counting determiners), one numeral adjective, one gerund functioning adjectivally, two nouns functioning as adjuncts, and one premodifying noun in the genitive case.

Bunyan's one sentence is a complex one consisting of three main clauses and three subordinate, of which two are adverbial and one adjectival.

Huxley's two sentences are both elliptic. 'Picture to yourself a squat grey building . . ' he might have said. 'Over the main entrance you can see in large letters . . . ', but he did not actually say these things because he felt such insertions to be needless. They would merely detract the reader's gaze from the firm features of that futuristic edifice which was destined in various ways to dominate his imaginary world.

Notice that Bunyan's one and only adjective is a particularizer. It echoes 'a certain' of the King James Bible, translating Gk *tis* (*topos tis* 'a certain place', Lat. *locus quidam*) which always followed its noun as an enclitic and which served as a substitute for the indefinite article in a language which possessed a definite article only.

Huxley's triad of abstractions echo cynically the three-word slogan of the French Revolution – actually much older than that Revolution – *liberté*, *égalité*, *fraternité*. The banners paraded through the streets of Paris on 13 May 1968 likewise bore a verbless triad followed by an adjective: *étudiants*, *enseignants*, *travailleurs solidaires*, referring, very significantly, to people, not abstractions.

INFLECTED AND PHRASAL GENITIVE

Aldous Huxley uses the inflected genitive 'World State's motto' and not the phrasal genitive 'motto of the World State' as both his famous grandfathers, Thomas Henry Huxley and Matthew Arnold, would doubtless have done in the nineteenth century. The English language retains in full use both the inflected genitive 'the king's son' corresponding to G *des Königs Sohn* and the phrasal genitive 'the son of the king' corresponding to F *le fils du roi*. Until recently, however, we inclined to limit inflected genitives to animate objects. As late as 1904 Henry Bradley wrote in *The Making of English*, Chapter 2: 'If we substitute the expression *England's history* for the more usual *the history of England*, we indicate that the name of the country is used with some approach to personification'. We have, it is true, long used the inflected genitive in expressions denoting duration of time and measure of distance: 'without one moment's delay', 'to give a week's notice', 'within a stone's throw', 'to reach journey's end'. We have also long used it in selected phrases like 'heart's ease' (still a countryman's name for the pansy), 'for my soul's health', 'in luck's way' and 'at the water's edge'. People say 'at the water's edge' in ordinary talk, but they do not say 'on the water's surface' or 'at the lake's edge' except in poetry. They prefer to say (without thinking much about it) 'on the surface of the water' and 'at the edge of the lake'. Until recently, they spoke indifferently of 'Shakespeare's plays' or 'the plays of Shakespeare', but they said 'the theatres of London' or 'London theatres', and not 'London's theatres'.

Today, however, this distinction between animate and

inanimate nouns is slowly disappearing. The inflected genitive is, after all, more succinct. 'The City's rush hour traffic jams' is shorter than 'traffic jams at the rush hour in the City'. 'Richmond's Mayor and Mayoress' is a pleasant variation on 'the Mayor and Mayoress of Richmond upon Thames'. 'The Sorbonne's rector' (*The Times*, 8 May 1968) is briefer, though less accurate, than 'the Rector of the University of Paris'. 'Today's weather forecast' sounds more snappy than 'the weather forecast for today'.

ATTRIBUTIVE GROUPS PRECEDING

The rule governing word order for attributives is a simple one: words come before, but groups follow.

> a squat grey building:
>> a building of thirty-four storeys
> a bright room:
>> a room with a view (novel by E. M. Forster, 1908)
> a private room:
>> a room of one's own (essay by Virginia Woolf, 1929)
> a robust man:
>> a man for all seasons (play by Robert Bolt, 1960)

Today, however, we observe a growing tendency, even to breaking point, to place attributive groups before the nouns they modify, making the meaning clear by means of hyphens in print and a different intonation in speech. Dickens did this when he made the one-eyed Bagman refer to his uncle Mr Jack Martin as 'a mighty free and easy, roving, devil-may-care sort of person' in Chapter 49 of *The Posthumous Papers of the Pickwick Club*.[1] Today we hear:

> an off-the-cuff opinion:
>> a viewpoint that is unofficial and unpremeditated

---

[1] See OED s.v. *Devil-may-care*, a., defined as the exclamation *devil may care!* used as an attributive meaning 'wildly reckless; careless and rollicking'.

off-the-record comments:
    observations that are not to be regarded as documentary
    or formal
round-the-clock discussions:
    discussions lasting some twelve hours
an often-referred-to book:
    a book that is frequently consulted
hard-to-get-at volumes:
    library tomes not readily accessible to readers
a who-does-what dispute:
    a trade union wrangle about which technician should do a
    particular job
a middle-of-the-road politician:
    a member of parliament who refrains from holding extreme
    views.

Hyphened phrasal verbs are also used in this position:
'drive-in banks', 'drive-on ferries', 'roll-on roll-off sea transport'.

The process is taken one stage further when the preceding
group is no longer hyphened:

    make or break year
    balance of payments deficit
    prices and incomes policy.

The Prime Minister was asked whether he considered flags of
convenience ships (= ships flying 'flags of convenience') to
have a lower standard than others (*The Times*, 30 March 1967).

SINGLE NOUN ADJUNCTS

World Court, the new title of the International Court of Justice
at The Hague, is a good example of a nominal group consisting
of head noun preceded by one noun adjunct. Its construction is
at once apparent only because in current English, as probably
long ago in IE, determinans precedes determinatum. This order
has been preserved in most IE derivative languages, but (for
reasons which need not now detain us) it has become reversed
in the Romance languages. We say *white house*, the Russians

belyj dom and the Germans *das weisse Haus*, whereas the French say *la maison blanche* and the Italians *la casa bianca*.

This simple fact – that in our language adjectives normally precede the nouns they modify – is of cardinal significance for the present and future development of nominal groups with single and multiple noun adjuncts. Here I am careful to say *normally*, and not *invariably*. Even in Old English the position of attributives was fairly flexible. Within fifty lines (727–776) of *Beowulf*, chosen at random, we encounter *leoht unfæger* 'ugly light', *wundor micel* 'a great marvel', and *medubenc monig* 'many a mead-bench'. Because it was feasible for Abbot Ælfric to say *regnscuras swete* as well as more normal *swete regnscuras* for 'sweet showers' in the tenth century, it was possible for Geoffrey Chaucer to say *shoures soote* as well as *soote shoures* in the fourteenth.[1] There was no syntactic discord. Even today, in our French-derived language of law, postmodifying attributives remain in *court martial, notary public, body politic, freehold absolute, heir apparent, heir presumptive, heir male, malice prepense* and *proof positive*.[2] In the field of military and civil organization we have recently acquired the formula head noun + adjunct in *Operation Dynamo* (evacuation from Dunkirk in June 1941), *Operation Overlord* (invasion of Normandy in June 1944), *Exercise Britannia* (implementation of Civil Defence), and *Enterprise Neptune* (preservation of British coasts sponsored by the National Trust).

Nevertheless, it is only because our basic order is determinans determinatum, and not the other way round, that such single and multiple nominal groups evade the perils of ambiguity. It is sometimes difficult to distinguish between genuine compounds and attributive constructions. Genuine compounds of

[1] Whan that Aprille with his shoures soote
The droghte of March hath perced to the roote . . .
General Prologue to the Canterbury Tales, I

[2] Absence of syntactic discord has been our great good fortune. Influences on our language have been manifold: Scandinavian, French, Latin through French, Latin direct, Greek through Latin through French, Greek through Latin, Greek direct, Low German, Italian and Spanish, but there has been no serious clash. We have been able to assimilate all these external influences without internal dissonance or disruption.

the tatpurusha type are ancient: OE *wordhord* 'vocabulary', *bordweall* 'phalanx', *heafodcirice* 'cathedral', *larhus* 'school', and so on. *Wonderloaf* and *Wheatsheaf*, the trade names of two of the biggest bread-producers in England, are compounds of this same type. On the other hand, *end product*, originally a technical term in chemistry, would seem to be a rendering of G *Endergebnis*.[1]

It is not always easy to distinguish between a compound noun like *earthquake* and a nominal group like *earth satellite*. The surest guides are stress and intonation, but these are often unstable. They may change in a few years. In any case, they vary with sentence rhythm. Moreover, on the semantic plane nominal groups become compounds when cohesion between components grows closer and more permanent. Nevertheless, for years, perhaps for centuries, compounds may carry a 'scintilla of ambiguity'. Do you make any distinction in stress and intonation between *headstone* marking the head of a grave and *head stone* denoting the principal stone in the foundation of a building?

In his famous speech on the futility of attempting to improve upon nature (*King John* IV ii 9), the Earl of Salisbury said 'taper light' instead of current 'taper's light' or 'light of a taper':

> *Therefore, to be possessed with double pomp,*
> *To guard a title that was rich before,*
> *To gild refined gold, to paint the lily,*
> *To throw a perfume on the violet,*
> *To smooth the ice, or add another hue*
> *Unto the rainbow, or with* taper light
> *To seek the beauteous eye of heaven to garnish,*
> *Is wasteful and ridiculous excess.*

Shakespeare was here using a nominal group very familiar to us now but very unfamiliar to a Tudor audience. Such nominal

---

[1] Its wide vogue probably arose from a popular television panel game called *What's My Line?* 'Is there an end product?' was a stock question in this game. For a short time in the late fifties *end product* threatened to oust *consequence, result, upshot, issue, outcome* and all its other synonyms from our vocabulary.

groups remained surprisingly rare in the seventeenth and eighteenth centuries. You will find very few in Johnson. Oliver Goldsmith preferred a premodifying genitive (in *The Captivity* II):

> *Hope, like the gleaming* taper's light,
> *Adorns and cheers our way;*
> *And still, as darker grows the night,*
> *Emits a brighter ray.*

It was not until the nineteenth century that the 'taper light' type of construction became common. Today the type proliferates unduly in such expressions as 'provision of recreation facilities', 'for health reasons', 'on efficiency grounds'. In 'wages award', 'weapons technology' and 'reparations payments' the adjunct is in the plural number. A yet more recent (and somewhat disturbing) development is the use of a premodifying noun attributive where a straightforward inflected genitive would be both more lucid and more accurate: 'Johnson warning to Egypt' (*The Times*, 25 May 1967), 'Callaghan remarks shock the house' (*The Times*, 21 February 1968), 'Rusk denial of note' (*The Times*, 3 September 1968). Perhaps 'Johnson warning', as contrasted with 'Johnson's warning', shows a slight shift from immediate reality towards cynical abstraction. A 'Johnson warning' is a peculiar Johnsonian type of warning. It is the kind of admonition that can emanate only from Mr Lyndon Baines Johnson, thirty-sixth President of the United States.

Verbless groups are not necessarily briefer than plain predications. The banner headline 'Wilson-Brown meeting: holidays interrupted by China crisis' has seventeen syllables in speech and fifty letters in writing. 'Wilson meets Brown: crisis in China interrupts holidays' is shorter by two syllables and three letters. In 1965 London Transport advertised for more staff by appealing to parents under the heading YOUR SON'S CAREER: 'He will be trained for a worthwhile future offering excellent promotional prospects', but the ending was infelicitous. To be frank, it was not always understood. In 1967, therefore, the last words were emended to read 'excellent prospects for promotion', with a carelessly chosen preposition. So, in 1968, a third shot was taken and, in the grammatical climate of that decade, its shape was inevitable. It had to take the form of a verbless nominal group: 'Sure employment with good prospects of promotion'.

MULTIPLE NOUN ADJUNCTS

As the number of premodifiers is increased from one to two or more, so meaning becomes more and more dependent upon context. *World Health Organization* is one of the eleven specialized agencies of the United Nations. It has no other possible point of reference. *Subscriber Trunk Dialling* designates that triumph of automation by which a private telephone subscriber can dial distant calls direct. A *Perimeter Security System* implies a particular arrangement of defences in the open space encircling a state prison to prevent the escape of dangerous criminals.

British historians still refer to the place of meeting between Henry VIII and Francis I of France in 1519 as the Field of the Cloth of Gold, and not Gold Cloth Field (G *Goldtuchfeld*) only because in his own language King Francis had no choice but to use the prepositional phrase *sur le champ de la toile d'or*.

When, in 1968, the trade union movement celebrated the lapse of one whole century since its foundation meeting at Manchester in 1868, its London headquarters in Great Russell Street displayed at its entrance the gigantic superscription TRADES UNION CONGRESS CENTENARY. Comprising one head noun and three premodifying adjunct nouns, this was indeed a characteristic nominal group. Obviously the premodifiers were not on a level. The immediate constituents were

Trades union congress|centenary,

and the mediate constituents

Trades union||congress|centenary.

Only as ultimate constituents could the closely cohering initial title be severed

Trades|||union||congress|centenary.

In the banner headline GUNTER RAIL PEACE PLAN,

similarly comprising one head noun and three premodifying adjunct nouns (*The Times*, 9 September 1967), the immediate constituents were

Gunter|rail peace plan,

the mediate constituents

Gunter|rail||peace plan

and the ultimate constituents

Gunter|rail||peace|||plan.

No one could comprehend this headline at first glance if he did not know that the Minister of Labour in those days was Mr Ray Gunter and that he was then pleading for reconciliation in the rail dispute about new duties arising from electrification.

OVERLOADED NOMINAL GROUPS

Premodifying nouns are serviceable preposition-saving devices, but three would seem to be their limit in the best interests of clarity and grace. Why pile Pelion upon Ossa? Why make communication unnecessarily laborious? Far too many sentences now lumber along heavily instead of tripping along lightly. This accumulation of attributes, to be sure, is now more fashionable than ever. 'You can date a passage,' observed that discerning cynic, Lord Edward Dunsany (1878–1957), 'by the frequency of multiple nouns and so can record our language decay progress.'

Every additional modifier makes some extra demand upon the reader's understanding. Let us take a simple instance, building up what linguists call a 'situational context'. Let us picture to ourselves a *station on a railway* (normal head noun with following attributive group). It is, in fact, a *railway station* (head noun with attributive noun preceding). This railway station has various offices and apartments, one of which is called a *waiting room* because there passengers can rest while they are *waiting* for a train. (Notice, by the way, that in this last sentence *waiting* performs two different grammatical roles: first as gerund functioning as premodifying noun adjunct, and secondly as present participle joined with the verb *to be* to form the present progressive tense.) This gives us a nominal group of four components:

railway station waiting room.

It so happens that this railway station is situated in a remote country district and that no one is near when two men meet in the waiting room and start up a political argument. Their quarrel leads to blows. One of the two men is killed:

railway station waiting room murder.

So, at least, it is reported in the local newspaper. But is it really murder, or only manslaughter? Did not the other man kill his opponent in self defence? Since no person actually witnessed the killing, Scotland Yard detectives are summoned to hold an investigation:

railway station waiting room murder inquiry.

In due course the formal investigation is held. Every available piece of evidence is collected and recorded. The relevant information is sedulously sifted from the irrelevant. All the resultant deductions are then weighed by judge and jury in the scales of probability against the killer's attestations made under oath. The judicial pronouncement is published:

railway station waiting room murder inquiry verdict.

Etymologically, as every lawyer knows, a verdict is *vere dictum* 'truly said'. But what is truth? said jesting Pilate, and would not stay for an answer. The prudent judge safeguards his verdict with the qualifying rider 'beyond all reasonable doubt' because experience has taught him that 'Time's slow finger' may later point to some odd fragment of hitherto unsuspected and unrevealed evidence which may prompt just men to challenge that decision of the court:

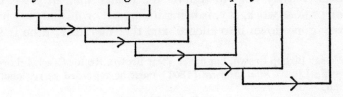

DESCRIPTIVE TITLES

On the whole we British have been hitherto highly selective in our employment of prefixed titles. Outside royalty and the nobility, the Church (Archbishop Matthew Parker, Archdeacon Grantly, Dean Swift),[1] the defence services (Admiral Venables, Colonel Hope, Wing Commander White), the police (Detective Superintendent Cass, Constable Ede), and local government (Alderman Day, Councillor Moore), British people have no high regard for prefixed titles. With Robert Burns they like to feel that

> *The rank is but the guinea's stamp;*
> *The man's the gowd (gold) for a' that.*

They like to feel that they are human beings, ordinary men and women, first of all.

Today, however, this attitude is changing. All kinds of titles and descriptive designations are being placed before proper names. You hear and read of Actress Mary Boon, Author Evelyn Waugh, and Immigration District Director Peter Esperdy. You hear and read of 'Foreign Secretary Michael Stewart' instead of 'Mr Michael Stewart, the Secretary of State for Foreign Affairs'; 'seventeen-year plumber's mate John Smith' instead of 'John Smith, a plumber's assistant, seventeen years of age'; 'Stone Brian Jones' instead of 'Mr Brian Jones, member of a group of popular entertainers called the Rolling Stones'; 'young Lambeth housewife Amy Green' instead of 'Mrs Green, a young Lambeth housewife'.

In literary circles it has long been customary to use the prefix Mr, Mrs or Miss if the person named is still alive. The present Poet Laureate is Mr Cecil Day-Lewis. His predecessor was John Masefield. This convention is both polite and practical. It may help to remind the reader that an artist or author (whose work, say, is being impugned or misjudged) has not yet 'gone down into silence' and that therefore, if he is so

---

[1] We say Bishop Brown, but never Vicar Brown. Rector Crackenthorpe in George Eliot's *Silas Marner* (1861) must be regarded as regionally dialectal.

minded, he can answer the challenge or rebut the charge on his own account. It is surely regrettable that this 'olde curteisye' is no longer carefully observed even in the quality press.

The downgrading of honorific titles has been a common tendency in many lands. In medieval England, for instance, the title *doctor* 'teacher' (Lat. *doceo, docēre* 'to teach') was assumed only by persons who had received from a university the attestation of their competence to lecture. As the teacher or doctor of medicine was the most widely known to people in general, the title came to be regarded as belonging more particularly to the physician. Later, in accordance with the tendency just mentioned to downgrade professional titles, it has come to be applied to any practitioner of the healing art, whether he has a university degree or not.

A dustman (binman in the north of England) now calls himself a *refuse collector*, and a ratcatcher a *rodent exterminator*, whereas a charwoman is now termed a *daily help* in the home and plain *cleaner* in a public building. A bookmaker or bookie (professional betting man at horse races) now advertises himself impressively as a *turf accountant* or *commission agent*, whereas a commercial traveller describes himself as a *sales representative*. He should not be confused with an *editorial representative* who, until recently, did good business as a literary agent. A night watchman figures as *security officer* on the company's payroll, whereas a constable of the initial grade will appear as a *police officer*, or even a *law-enforcement officer*, in press reports. Have railway station masters risen in prestige since they became *station managers*? This revised title will, let us hope, encourage closer and more businesslike relations with other members of the station staff.

Meantime the title of *chairman* continues to rise in status. In Tudor England this appellation was still unknown for the simple reason that control by committee was unknown in that autocratic society. The earliest recorded instance of this simple compound occurs characteristically during Cromwell's Protectorate, though casually enough in John Trapp's *Commentary upon Job* (1654). Today *chairman* is used by foreign correspondents to translate not only Russian *predsedatel*, the chief executive officer of the Soviet Union, but also *i chang*, the titular head of the Chinese People's Republic.

A Company Chairman presides over its Board of Directors, shoulders the heaviest burden of responsibility, reports direct to shareholders, and generally draws the highest salary. The Chairman of Committees in either House of Parliament is the member appointed to preside over it whenever it resolves itself into committees, but the permanent chairman of the House of Commons remains the Speaker.

What happens if the person elected to preside over a meeting is a woman? Current convention requires that she too be called chairman and not *chairwoman* which sounds too much like *charwoman*. (In some dialects, to be sure, the two words are homophones.) Instead of Mr Chairman she is addressed, oddly enough, as Madam Chairman.

LOSS OF FEMININE SUFFIXES

The emancipation of women, the advent of cheap motor cars, and the invention of television mark the three greatest social changes of our day. All three touch language closely.

Emancipation implies not only 'equal pay for equal work', but also equal status. Differentiating titles therefore find little favour. *Authoress*, for instance, tends to be discarded. *Poetess*, on the other hand, is frequently retained with full honours. Elsewhere difficulties may arise. The conductor of an orchestra may be a woman, but for obvious reasons the female conductor of a bus is designated *conductress*. It is not easy to dispense with the suffix *-ess* as applied to a *waitress* in a restaurant, a *stewardess* on an air liner, a *manageress* of a hotel, an *actress* on the stage, or a *patroness* of the fine arts. A woman ambassador, however, may not call herself *ambassadress* for that is the title conferred upon an ambassador's wife; nor can a woman mayor call herself *mayoress* for that is a separate office to be held by one of her relatives. Nor can we extend the masculine gender to pronouns and possessive adjectives if they relate to females. We have no choice but to refer to a woman mayor as *she* or *Her Worship*. And what do we do when a Lord Mayor is a woman? *Lady Mayor* suggests a horse. A northern port has just solved the problem (or evaded the issue) by finding nothing incongruous in referring to its First Citizen, who happens to be of the fair sex, as *Her Worship the Lord Mayor of Liverpool*. All the more reason why we should honour all noble ladies from *Duchess*, *Marchioness* and *Countess* to *Viscountess* and *Baroness*. Since the institution of Life Peers in 1958, a Baroness may be a commoner of merit upon whom the baronial title has been conferred for services performed.

In recent years, half playfully, we have toyed with such derivatives as *announcerette*, *conductorette*, *stewardette*, and many others. *Undergraduette*, it is true, enjoyed some vogue at Oxford in the twenties when women were first admitted to the degrees of that ancient university. Henry Cecil Wyld, who was there at the time, refused outright to include it in his *Universal Dictionary* of 1932, but Onions admitted it to the First OED Supplement of the following year, whence it passed into most British and American dictionaries of any size or standing. Onions, somewhat surprisingly, found room for *undergraduette* in his highly selective ODEE of 1966, at the same time marking it down as 'irregular'. Of all these experimental feminine derivatives, *usherette* (in a cinema) is the only one to be taken sufficiently seriously to enable it to survive.

CHAPTER 6

Verbs and Verbal Groups

THE MOST extensive changes in current English usage are those affecting verbs and verbal groups. Although verbs have lost most of their inflexions except - (e)s, - ing, - (e)d or - (e)n, they have more than made up for this by the development of other means of expressing the most subtle refinements of tense, aspect, and modality. It is not my intention at this point to deal systematically with the deep structure of these changes, but rather to focus attention on single features. You will probably find this method both easier to follow and more stimulating to the imagination. You will certainly have observed many of these changes actually taking place in the speech you hear around you day by day and you will find it good fun to supplement the illustrative examples with even better ones from your own recent experience.

GROWING USE OF PROGRESSIVE FORMS

Progressive forms consist of some tense of the substantive verb *to be* followed immediately by the present or first participle. They denote that an action, happening or state is actually in progress, is of short duration, or is vividly pictured in the mind of the speaker.

	Simple	*Progressive*
Present	do	am doing
Present Perfect	have done	have been doing
Past	did	was doing
Past Perfect	had done	had been doing
Future	shall do	shall be doing
Future Perfect	shall have done	shall have been doing

Progressive forms are concerned with both *aspect* and *tense*. Aspect expresses the speaker's attitude towards the completion or incompletion of an action, whereas tense expresses his attitude towards its time or timelessness. Together with *mood*, *mode*, or *modality*, aspect and tense constitute the three primary verbal categories. Mood expresses the speaker's attitude towards the actuality, or degree of hypothesis or supposition, associated with an action, happening or state.

The differences between the traditional uses of simple and progressive forms can be shown by means of contrasted sentences, (a) expressing an unqualified action or state, and (b) expressing limited duration.

(a) I live in London: my home is there
(b) I am living in London for the next three weeks

(a) My uncle finds fault with everything I do
(b) My uncle is for ever finding fault

(a) Wait until the train stops
(b) This train is stopping at all stations

(a) I read Russian as well as French and German
(b) I am reading *Anna Karenina*

(a) John plays tennis on Saturday afternoons
(b) John is not at home: he is playing tennis

(a) Mary is now five, and she goes to school
(b) Mary is in a hurry: she is going to school

Unfortunately, these useful distinctions are no longer (being) strictly observed. You hear people say 'John is playing tennis on Saturday afternoons' when he is, in fact, at this moment pruning his roses; and you hear them say 'Mary is going to school now' when she is, in fact, at this moment watching television.

Until recently many verbs expressing mental states and attitudes – *believe, forget, hate, hear, hope, imagine, know, like, love, mean, remember, seem, smell, taste*, and *understand* – were seldom or never used in their progressive forms. This remains generally true in principle and it is good to teach such a list to foreign students who will then ask 'What do you believe?' and not 'What are you believing?', 'What does he really know?' and not 'What is he really knowing?', 'Do they like sugar with their tea?' and not 'Are they liking sugar . . .?'

The simple present is still employed to state universal truths, and it is then sometimes called the *timeless present*:

The sun rises in the east

Water freezes at 0° centigrade
as against

The sun is rising over Tower Bridge

The water in the Round Pond is freezing

The simple present is also used in stage directions, when it is termed the *dramatic present*:

Macbeth welcomes Duncan to his castle
The Hall of David Bliss's house is very comfortable and extremely untidy

It is also used to vivify past events, when it is termed the *historic present*:

Napoleon retreats from Moscow
The Treaty of Rome is signed

Why is it that progressive forms are otherwise increasing at the expense of simple forms? After all, the latter are shorter and more economical; but people desire, often vaguely and subconsciously, to make what they say (are saying) more lively and vivid.

When you *were talking* about making No. 10 (Downing Street) a power house and not a monastery, you *were* really *meaning* that you wanted to strengthen both No. 10 and the Cabinet Secretariat
   Mr Norman Hunt in a broadcast interview with the Prime Minister, recorded in *The Listener*, 6 April 1967

It is Frank Ramsey who comes back most vividly to my mind when I speak of the Heretics (Society at Cambridge). I *am remembering* an occasion when, as secretary of the society, he read from the minute book a very learned and complete summary of a philosophical lecture . . . but the pages were blank.

Kingsley Martin, *Father Figures* (1966) p. 108

All the people in this programme *are remembering* the days of their childhood
BBC Radio 4 23 June 1968

The matron (at Guy's Hospital) does not know all she *should be knowing* about this affair
BBC 2 Television Newsroom 3 July 1968

It is not at all clear what the Chancellor *is meaning* by that last statement
We have learnt much from this White Paper and we *are* all *understanding* the situation better now
My son *is hoping* to spend Easter in Switzerland
Grandpa *is forgetting* names nowadays
You *are* surely *imagining* things

Compare Southern English 'I'm listening' with Scottish 'I hear you' signifying 'Yes, I hear every word you say. You have made your point, but I have no further comment to make at the moment.'

In some ways this supersession of simple by progressive forms can be regarded as the continuation of a long process. Progressive forms are not new. They were used by the nameless author of *Beowulf* and by King Alfred in his translations, especially when rendering deponentia like *passus est* 'wæs ðrowiende' and *locutus est* 'wæs sprecende'. They were used by Shakespeare, but not frequently. Whereas, for instance, the boatswain (in *The Tempest* I i 41) asks Sebastian 'What do you here?' one would now say 'What are you doing here?' And whereas Polonius (in *Hamlet* II ii 195) asks 'What do you read, my lord?' one would now say 'What are you reading, my lord?' 'Any Mans death diminishes me', wrote John

Donne, 'because I am involved in Mankinde; And therefore never send to know for whom the bell tolls, It tolls for thee'.[1] In modern parlance one would say 'Do not trouble to ask who that passing bell is ringing for. It is ringing for you'. It was during the last years of the Second World War that this impressive peroration achieved wide renown, due partly, no doubt, to the popularity of Ernest Hemingway's autobiographical novel *For Whom the Bell Tolls* (1941) describing four eventful days in the Spanish Civil War. 'I am involved in Mankinde', echoing Terence's 'Homo sum: humani nil a me alienum puto', was adopted as a watchword by the humanists. *Involvement* became a vogue word.

One important use of the progressive present is to express immediately future time:

We are moving shortly into a larger house
Our guests are leaving tomorrow early
Mr Smith is resigning from the chairmanship (implying that he has not yet handed in his formal resignation, but that he will probably do so in the near future).

Going to EXPRESSING THE NEAR FUTURE

We can now express the immediate future in several ways:

> Mr Smith is resigning
>   to resign
>   on the point of resigning
>   about to resign
>   going to resign

All five are in current use, but the last is now by far the commonest. Indeed, in spite of occasional protests in letters addressed to the daily newspapers and elsewhere against 'the utterly irrational misuse of this precious little verb of motion', *going to* + infinitive is rapidly becoming the normal catenative for the expression of the immediate future. What is time? Can

---

[1] Meditation 17, A.D. 1624. See John Donne, *Selected Sermons*, ed. Evelyn M. Simpson, p. 243.

you define it? You can, perhaps, more readily visualize it as a horizontal line along which a point (the present moment) moves from left to right.

> *Hear the voice of the Bard,*
> *Who present, past and future, sees;*
> *Whose ears have heard*
> *The Holy Word*
> *That walked among the ancient trees.*

So sang William Blake in the Introduction to his *Songs of Experience* and modern man agrees with him in conceiving time as tripartite. Modern man is much concerned with that ever moving point on the line of time. One recent manifestation of this concern is to be seen in the adoption into daily life of that twenty-four hour system of four figures (0001 to 2400) which has long been customary in the defence services. 'Don't get caught up in the rushes. Shop between 1000 and 1600.' This monitory advertisement, addressed primarily to housewives, first appeared in 1967.[1] In that same year synchronized indicators, displaying hours and minutes in four figures, began to replace clocks on railway stations and other public buildings.

Our ancestors, less obsessed than we by the passing minute, thought of time as twofold: past and non-past. The present-future was indeed the non-past, conceived as one. In Old English, therefore, as in Indo-European, there was no future tense. Even the mantic or vatic future was expressed by the present tense. So, for example, the disembodied voice (in Abbot Ælfric's translation of *Daniel* IV 32) has no other choice in addressing Nebuchadnezzar, King of Babylon, than to use the plain present: *þu itst gærs, swa swa oxa, seofon gear* 'thou eatest (= shalt eat) grass, like an ox, seven years'.

In Ewe, an African Negro language spoken in Togoland and part of the Gold Coast, and in certain Amerindian languages, the same word denotes 'yesterday' and 'tomorrow' as 'not today'. Oddly enough, Gothic *gistradagis*, cognate with our *yesterday*, occurring only once (*Matthew* VI 30) in Bishop

---

[1] Wordplay on two meanings of rush: (1) waterside plant; (2) peak-hour traffic.

Wulfila's Bible, means 'tomorrow'. In other European languages expressions for 'the morrow' come from words meaning 'morning' (F *demain*, Ital. *domani*, Sp. *mañana*, G *morgen*). The semantic shift is easy to trace from 'in the morning' to 'on the following morning' to 'on the following day'.

Some IE languages developed their own specific inflexions for the future tense in accordance with the axiomatic linguistic principle that, when need arises, *Homo loquens* will always 'find out the way' to satisfy it. From *ama bhu* 'to love I grow', Latin evolved *amābō*. From *aimer ai* 'to love I have' French evolved *aimerai*. Unlike Latin and French, English has not employed such suffixes as it might have done if *I have to go* (page 132) expressing objective compulsion or necessity, had been transposed as *I go have (to)*, and had subsequently been somehow coalesced into one word. Instead of this, English has made use of the auxiliary verbs *shall*, *will* and *worth*. It was indeed unfortunate that *worth* early fell into desuetude, whereas *werden*, its German counterpart, has been preserved to this day. In this respect German has been luckier than English which has been driven to use *shall* 'owe, be indebted' and *will* 'intend' as its two competing auxiliaries of the future tense. The differences in semantic colouring between them have become neutralized in familiar speech where both are reduced to a dark *l* in pronunciation. 'I'll [ail] be there' stands in Southern English for both 'I shall be there' (future time) and 'I will be there' (personal intention). Today 'I'm going to be there' means much the same, expressing, as we have just seen, a gentle intention for the immediate future. Here *go* has quite lost its old meaning *walk* as contrasted with *run, jump, creep, slide, ride, swim* and *fly*.[1] In the statement 'I am going to go' this two-letter verb functions as its own catenative. You may recall that witty allusion to Mr Pecksniff's horse in *Martin Chuzzlewit* (1844): 'He was full of promise, but of no performance. He was always, in a manner, going to go, and never going.'

This use of 'going to' (slang *gounta* and *gonna* [gənə]) is,

---

[1] The sense 'walk' was long preserved in *go-cart*, a Victorian contraption consisting of a framework on rollers designed to help children to walk. See ODEE s.v. *go*.

by the way, much older than Dickens. In its initial stages it is found in Shakespeare. When, for instance, the Duke of Vienna (in *Measure for Measure* III i 194), disguised as a friar, asks Isabella how on earth she can ever hope to save her brother Claudio, she tells him that she is actually on her way to see Claudio in order to dispel his doubts and fears: 'I am now going to resolve him'. And when Escalus in the scene following (III ii 241) declares 'I am going to visit the prisoner', he means not 'I intend to visit him' but 'I am now actually on my way'. It is easy to see how, in certain situational contexts, the difference between these two meanings may become negligible, but the important point to observe here is that Shakespeare employs this expression very rarely indeed. In all his plays and poems you will not find more than eight examples whereas in *Oliver Twist* alone you will find 24 instances (nearly 4 per cent) of *going to* as against 650 of *shall* and *will*. One century later, in Jeremy David Salinger's *The Catcher in the Rye* (1951), you will find 75 instances (over 30 per cent) of *going to* as against 240 of *shall* and *will*.[1] An early instance of *going to*, expressing a negative intention in the first person, occurs in a letter from Charlotte Brontë to her friend Ellen in 1855:

> I must write one line out of my dreary bed . . . I am not going to talk of my sufferings – it would be useless and painful.[2]

> If it is fine this evening, I am going to paint my garden shed
> We are certainly not going to tolerate any nonsense from that quarter

Only in the third person does *going to* express a colourless future:

> Lord Woolton is going to be a very serious loss to the party
> *Observer* 9 October 1955
> According to the forecast, the weather is going to remain dry
> The new hospital is going to cost one million pounds

[1] For these statistics I am indebted to Dr Jana Molhova of the University of Sofia.
[2] See Elizabeth Cleghorn Gaskell's *Life of Charlotte Brontë*, p. 522.

It is going to be difficult to track down the cause of this disaster

Nothing is going to happen

AUXILIARIES AND ANOMALOUS FINITES

Verbs are divided into two classes: finites and non-finites. The finites likewise fall into two categories: full and auxiliary. Full finites and non-finites are countless, but the auxiliaries are twelve in number:

Primary	be, have, do
Modal	shall, will, can, may, must, ought
Marginal	dare, need, used

Never in the history of English have these twelve innocent monosyllables played such an important part in speech as they do today.

It is important to observe that the term *auxiliary* refers to function, whereas *anomalous finite* refers to form. Thus these terms are by no means convertible. The former is the traditional one applied to the one dozen verbs just mentioned, whereas the latter was invented by Harold Edward Palmer to denote the two dozen forms of verbs that appear in the following table:

Primary	am, is, are	was, were
	have, has	had
	do, does	did
Modal	shall	should
	will	would
	can	could
	may	might
	must	
	ought (to)	
Marginal	need	
	dare	
		used (to)

All eleven forms in the first group are both full and auxiliary verbs. Those in the second group (with the exception of *will* in 'It shall be as you will') are auxiliary verbs only. Those in the third group, as we shall see later, are slowly losing their function and status as auxiliary verbs.

These twenty-four finites have four important characteristics in current speech:

(a) they, and they alone, form negatives in *n't*:

You haven't the required qualifications

or You don't hold the required qualifications

but not *You holdn't the required qualifications

The children won't stay any longer

or The children don't want to stay any longer

but not *The children wantn't to stay any longer

(b) they change places with the subject after an initial negation or its equivalent:

Never have I seen lovelier roses than these

Not once has he faltered

Seldom do we find time to go swimming

Little did they know that they were being watched

(c) they are used in simple questions as follows:

Is it?

or Does it exist?

but not *Exists it?

Have you the money?

or Do you possess the money?

but not *Possess you the money?

Must you go now?

Ought we to tell him?

Could anyone have been passing at the time?

(d) they, and they alone, are employed in question tags, both positive and negative:

We all agree on this, don't we?

We don't disagree, do we?

You will do your best, won't you?

You won't let the side down, will you?

It is now highly fashionable to collocate anomalous finites with a view to conveying special emphasis or producing stylistic effects:

> The number of entrants to universities has increased as the Robbins Report said it *could* and *should*
> > *The Listener* 9 December 1965

> All those contributing to this book have a very practical interest in all that *does*, *might*, or *should* go on in higher education
> > *Oxford* December 1965

> Violent disturbances of the balance of power *can* and *do* and *will* take place even when the interests of major nuclear powers are at stake
> > *The Listener* 17 February 1966

> Nature is wonderfully resilient, but man, out of self-interest and a sense of responsibility, *can* and *should* do more to help
> > *Radio Times* 21 April 1966

Sometimes, alas, constructions are maladjusted:

> That argument *can* too easily and *has* too often been used to stifle discussion
> > *The Times Business News* 24 May 1968

Read 'can too easily be'.

Sentence patterns hinging on these two dozen anomalous finites are fairly stable for all except the last three, *dare*, *need* and *used*, which I have therefore called *marginal*. Like the three primaries *am*, *have* and *do*, these also function as full verbs. But whereas the primaries are in such frequent use that full and auxiliary functions are easily kept distinct in different sentence patterns, the marginals are so rarely employed that auxiliary uses and functions are gradually forgotten. Instead of 'John daren't risk it', 'Dare we take the risk?', 'You needn't go', and 'Need you ask?', people tend to say 'John doesn't dare to risk it', 'Do we dare to take the risk?', 'You don't need to go', 'Do

you need to ask?' The most untidy of the three marginals is
used, which few speakers, even the most careful ones, now
employ as a genuine auxiliary:

Used you to play rugby at school?
No, I used not.
But you used to play some game, usen't you?
Of course I used to: soccer in winter, cricket and tennis in
summer.

Almost invariably we now hear:

Did you use to play rugby at school?
No, I did not.
But you used to play some game, didn't you?
Of course I did: soccer in winter, cricket and tennis in
summer.

Here *did* in 'I did not', 'didn't you?' and 'of course I did' is the
pro-verb or *verbum vicarium* which enables the speaker to avoid
the repetition of a verb just as a pronoun saves him from
repeating a noun. Usage demands that *do*, our one and only
pro-verb, does not stand in the place of an auxiliary:

You play, don't you?
or   You would play, wouldn't you?
but not * You would play, don't you?

When Milton (in *Lycidas* 67) employed this marginal
anomalous finite in the present tense –

> *Were it not better done, as others* use
> *To sport with Amaryllis in the shade*
> *Or with the tangles of Neaera's hair?*

– he was making use of a form that was already archaic. It is
surely not surprising that most children, citing these famous
lines, now say –

> *Were it not better done, as others* do

– with no loss to sound and rhythm, and little loss to sense. The
plain fact that *used to* [ju:stu] has long been employed in the

E

past tense only has certainly jeopardized its survival as one of Palmer's neat array of two dozen anomalous finites.

The question, therefore, whether *didn't use to* is substandard has now become an open one. It is certainly not on a level with *didn't ought* in which *ought* is made to function as an infinitive, or with *hadn't ought* in which *ought* is made to function no less maladroitly as a second participle. Nevertheless, the latter was given wide popularity by Francis Bret Harte in his poem *Mrs Judge Jenkins*:

> *If, of all words of tongue and pen,*
> *The saddest are, ' It might have been',*
> *More sad are these we daily see:*
> *' It is, but hadn't ought to be.'*

The northern 'grammatical isogloss' of *hadn't ought* is shown by Raven I. McDavid as passing westward from the mouth of the Delaware River through Pennsylvania, Ohio and Indiana.[1] Meantime other strange collocations like *might could* and *used to could* are gaining currency even among educated speakers in the southern States:

> If Smith had the necessary dollars, he might could pull it off
> When I was younger I used to could, but no longer now[2]

HAVE YOU ANY?

Until recently a convenient distinction was made between (a) 'Have you any?' referring to a permanent possession or attribute, and (b) 'Do you have any?' referring to something occasional or habitual.

> (a) Baa, baa, black sheep,
>   Have you any wool?

> *Old Nursery Rhyme*

[1] See W. Nelson Francis, *The Structure of American English*, New York, Ronald Press 1958, p. 583.

[2] Is it possible that Pennsylvania Dutch has helped to foster such anomalies? I recall reading 'he should have ought to come' as a rendering of *er hätte kommen sollen* in a German textbook.

Has Mary blue eyes?
Have you any HP7 batteries (to sell to me now)?
We have a few trees in our garden
Had they much money?

(b) Does Mary have many friends?
Do you have HP7 batteries (in stock)?
We do not have many visitors at the weekend
Did they have much trouble?

This distinction is no longer observed partly because it is not always a clear distinction and partly because the *do*-construction falls into line with that governing other full verbs.

What is charm? It's a sort of bloom on a woman. If you have it, you don't need to have anything else; and if you don't have it, it doesn't much matter what else you have
Sir James Barrie, *What Every Woman Knows*, Act I

This is well said. It would be pointless to insist on substituting 'you need not have' because this is the proper construction with a marginal anomalous finite, or to insist on changing to 'if you haven't (got) it' on the ground that feminine charm is an attribute.

When, however, in 1966 an insurance company displayed an advertisement beneath an exceptionally attractive picture of happy children at play, some people found the wording faulty:

There was a time when you didn't have a care in the world. If things have changed a little since then, have a word with the SUN ALLIANCE

People criticized the wording because 'I haven't a care in the world' is an old popular saying. The advertiser should certainly have said 'There was a time when you hadn't a care' since his sole aim was to echo this old saying and to evoke the image of a golden childhood.

Compare 'Have you?' and 'Do you have?' with 'Are you?' and *'Do you be?', 'Do you?' and 'Do you do?' Will *'Do you be?' ever become standard English? At the moment it is regionally dialectal, but the *do*-construction is already standard in negative interrogatives:

> Why don't you be a good boy?
> Why on earth doesn't the fellow be reasonable?

As a formal greeting 'How do you?' = 'How prosper you?' survived into the early nineteenth century when only younger people said 'How do you do?'[1] Nevertheless, people now say 'and what have you', not 'and what do you have' instead of 'and so on, and what not' at the end of an uncompleted list. Little by little, we even detect *do* coming into use as the pro-verb of *have*:

> John has a fine library, and so do I
> Some have good manners, and some do not

USES OF GET, GOT

The strengthening of a weakly stressed *have* by a strongly stressed *got* is now customary not only with the full verb *have* in 'I have got no time' but also with modal *have to* in 'I have got to go now', expressing external necessity. We detect a gradual crescendo or orchestration from *am to go* (suggesting that my going is down, as it were, on some programme) to *ought to go* (implying that my going is something in the nature of a Kantian categorical imperative):

> I am to go
> have to go
> have got to go
> must go
> should go
> ought to go

In the past tense 'I have (got) to go' and 'I must go' now share one common form 'I had to go'. *Had to* is therefore said to be the past tense analogue of *must*. Context will determine the precise degree of obligation or necessity. When Ada Galsworthy

---

[1] OED, s.v. *do*, v. 19.

said to her husband, 'You ought to write. You are just the person', she implied no strong sense of impelling duty. *Should*, expressing moral obligation, is increasing at the expense of *must* and *ought: have got to*, expressing objective necessity, is increasing at the expense of *am to* and plain *have to*. Meantime, too, constructions with get + participle are growing abundantly:

(a) *get* + first participle, especially in the imperative:
   Get going! Get cracking! Get weaving!
   No strike here! Get together and get talking!

(b) *get* + object + second participle:
   To get things started, get things done, get a book published, get the car overhauled, get the house cleaned up and decorated, get wrongs righted, get justice done

(c) *get* + second participle alone:
   To get born, brought up, educated, married, promoted, dismissed, spotted, killed

People now say 'We got caught in a heavy shower', and not, as in the nineteenth century and before, 'We were caught'. They say 'We don't want to be involved', and not 'We do not wish to be implicated'. *Want*, by the way, is rapidly supplanting *wish* and *desire*. Like *get*, it is a northern monosyllable from Scandinavian. Its earlier meaning 'lack' is preserved in the proverb 'Waste not, want not'.

Keep PLUS FIRST PARTICIPLE

Both *get going* 'begin to go' and *keep going* 'continue to go' are of recent origin. The earliest known recorded instance of the latter construction occurs in William Gifford's *Baviad* of 1794. There he censured *keep moving* as a 'contemptible vulgarity'.[1] In the nineteenth century 'Keep smiling' remained long in favour as a friendly greeting and Lena Guilbert Ford's *Keep the home fires burning* cheered the hearts of fighting men in the First

---

[1] OED s.v. *keep*, v. 40b.

World War. Today *keep on* is the commonest of all catenative
verbs:

> Why does that dog keep on barking?
> It kept on raining all day long
> Untended cattle will keep on breaking down the hedges
> Keep on keeping on[1]

GERUND FOR INFINITIVE

The gerund continues to grow at the expense of the infinitive.
Whereas, for instance, Baptista (in *The Taming of the Shrew*
III ii 27) says to Katharina 'I cannot blame thee now to weep',
one would now say 'for weeping'; and whereas Elizabeth
Woodville (in *Richard II* II ii 34) asks distractedly 'Oh, who
shall hinder me to wail and weep?', one would now say 'from
wailing and weeping'; and whereas Beatrice (in *Much Ado
About Nothing* IV i 293) taunts Benedick with 'You kill me to
deny it', one would now say 'in denying it'.

The gerund expresses an action as a process: the infinitive
merely names an action. Both gerund and infinitive are verbal
nouns. Their spheres inevitably overlap and, since Shakespeare's day, there has been a general drift towards the gerund.
Very often the speaker has an open choice without appreciable
differentiation in meaning:

> When do you propose making (to make) a start?
> Dickens continued publishing (to publish) his stories in
> serial form
> I have few opportunities of seeing (to see) live theatre
> Our visitors preferred walking (to walk) home
> I like listening (to listen) to orchestral music
> The Government cannot escape the choice between hitting
> both imports and employment . . . as Mr Wilson took three
> years finding (to find) out
> *The Times Business News* 30 August 1968

---

[1]Former motto of the Salvation Army.

Sometimes, however, as with the verbs *begin, try* and *remember*, the two forms diverge in meaning:

(a) John began learning French as a child of seven (marking the start of a long process)

(b) There was a lightning flash and it began to thunder (indicating inchoative aspect)

(a) Try standing up (as an experiment, said to a healthy man doing a new kind of job)

(b) Try to stand up (as a special effort, said to a sick man getting out of bed)

(a) Can you remember locking your car? (referring to past time)

(b) You must remember to lock your car (referring to future time)

One cause of the increased use of the gerund lies in the fact that it must be employed after all prepositions except *to*:

We gave up going (ceased to go) to the races when my grandfather died

Mary refrained from saying (forbore to say) what she really thought in her heart

Do not put off having (fail to have) your car overhauled before leaving (before you decide to leave)

It is interesting to observe that the gerund remains neutral in diathesis or voice. being neither active nor passive:

That needs explaining (to be explained)

The tale lost nothing in the telling (in being told)

This whole place requires tidying up

Such things do not bear thinking about

What is worth doing at all is worth doing well

PHRASAL VERBS

A phrasal verb is a verbal group consisting of a verb closely linked with one or more adverbs or prepositions. If we call the latter particles we need no longer distinguish between them.

For instance, *across* can be called a particle in both 'John came across to me' (adverb) and 'John came across the road' (preposition). We call *came across* a phrasal verb because verb and particle form one unit. Instead of *came across* we can say *crossed*. Moreover, we can use this phrasal verb in a special or metaphorical sense:

> John came across (found by chance) an old manuscript in the lumber room
> As I was roaming over the moor I came across (happened to discover) an ancient tumulus

Phrasal verbs are characteristic of the Germanic languages. You will find few in the Romance or Slavonic tongues. Some English writers, like Johnson and Gibbon, use them rarely. Try reading at random any one chapter of *Rasselas* and any one chapter of the *History of the Decline and Fall of the Roman Empire* and see how many you can discover. Perhaps you will find none at all, whereas in today's newspaper you will encounter several on every page.

Phrasal verbs are now proliferating at every level. People say 'I give it up' (G *ich gebe es auf*) rather than 'I abandon it' (F *Je l'abandonne*). As with the inflected and phrasal genitives (see p. 105) we here have two choices, whereas German and French have one each. We call *aufgeben* a separable verb because the prefix (formerly a preposition) and the root are regularly separated in certain positions but brought together again in others, separated in *ich gebe es auf* but combined in *Ich muss den Plan aufgeben* 'I must the plan up-give' and *Das ist der Plan den ich unglücklicherweise aufgab* 'That is the plan which I unfortunately up-gave'.

We have nothing quite like this in English, but we have something approaching it in the different uses with, say, *run-up* (phrasal verb, consisting of verb + adverb) and *run up* (non-phrasal, consisting of verb + preposition):

> The signalmen ran up (hoisted) the flag
> or The signalmen ran the flag up
> The children ran up the lane
> but not *The children ran the lane up

You must keep down (minimize) expenses

or   You must keep expenses down

You must keep down this road

but not *You must keep this road down

John turned off (extinguished) the light

or   John turned the light off

John turned off the main road

but not *John turned the main road off

The builder's foreman looked over (inspected) the wall

or   The builder's foreman looked the wall over

The boy looked over the wall

but not *The boy looked the wall over

We may perhaps begin our survey of phrasal verbs by listing all the verbs and particles most frequently combined in their formation. It so happens that the verbs, about two dozen of them, are all monosyllabic, and so are the fifteen or so particles with the exception of *about, across* and *over*. The verbs are, in alphabetical order, *back, blow, break, bring, call, catch, come, fall, get, give, go, hold, keep, lay, let, look, make, put, run, set, stand, take, turn* and *work* combining with the particles *about, across, at, by, down, for, in, off, on, out, over, round, through, to* and *up.*

The resultant combinations can be grouped into three categories as follows: (1) The verb and the particle more or less retain their separate meanings although (as in *came across = crossed*, just mentioned) they are joined to express one thought or action. Such are *bring forth* (produce), *call on* (visit), *come upon* (encounter), *get away* (escape), *get back* (recover), *go into* (enter), *hold up* (obstruct), *keep back* (retain), *look over* (inspect, survey), *put off, take off* (doff), *put on* (don), *put out* (dout, extinguish), *set up* (establish, organize), *step up* (escalate); (2) The verb alone retains its meaning, but that meaning is in some way modified or intensified by the particle which has lost much or all of its own particular signification: *break up* (end the school term), *find out* (discover), *give up* (abandon, cease trying), *leave off* (stop, desist), *look after* (supervise), *work out* (calculate); (3) The verb and the particle both lose their separate identities and acquire new senses when they become closely linked: *bring up* (nurse, educate), *carry out* (execute), *carry through* (complete), *come by* (obtain), *get by* (manage, make do), *get up* (arrange), *give in* (succumb, surrender), *go into* (investigate), *keep up* (maintain), *make out* (understand), *put off* (postpone), *take in* (deceive), *take off* (mimic, ridicule by imitation), *take over* (assume control), *turn out* (develop, evolve), *turn up* (appear, as if by chance).

It must be conceded that many phrasal verbs in Group 1 are not easy to distinguish from simple verb + particle. The transition may be a gentle one, as seen in such sequences as the following:

John called on the secretary to read his report
John called on (visited) the secretary later in the evening

Mary laughed at tea time
Mary laughed at that point in the story
Mary laughed at the joke
Mary laughed at (mocked) me

Orpheus looked round the corner
Orpheus looked round to see whether Eurydice was following him
Orpheus descended into the underworld to look round (make reconnaissance, examine the situation)

Many phrasal verbs will, in fact, belong to both Groups 1 and 3 according to literal or metaphorical use:

We could not go into (enter) the room because the door was locked

We could not go into (investigate) the problem because the evidence was not forthcoming

The cricket team got up (rose) early to catch a train
The cricket team got up (arranged) a dance to defray expenses

John was taken in (accommodated for the night) by a friend
John was taken in (swindled) by a crook

I cannot make out (write) a cheque because I have no pen
I cannot make out (decipher, interpret) this inscription
because I have no light

Some of these senses are old: others are surprisingly recent.
There are still feckless folk in the world who, like Mr Wilkins
Micawber in *David Copperfield*; like, indeed, Dickens's own
father, jog along from day to day waiting hopefully for something to *turn up*. This expression is, then, over one century old,
but if you consult the OED you will find that the earliest
recorded instance of this use of *turn up* (sense *v*) is dated 1704
and that this metaphorical sense derives from a game of cards.

There are other kinds of people in the world who are quite
content to *get by* 'manage, make do, get along somehow'. I
first heard this expression in 1955, but then, for a brief period,
it seemed to be on everyone's lips. What was my surprise,
therefore, to find it actually recorded in the OED Supplement
of 1933! It is there defined as intransitive 'to be successful in
escaping or evading something; to succeed, manage; to get
away with, originally U.S. colloq(uial)'. Since 1933 the latter
has been generally followed by the indefinite pronoun. *To get
away with it* now signifies 'to act with impunity, evade
retribution, succeed in one's (not always scrupulous) plans'.

That equating of *get by* with *get away with* may serve to
remind us that phrasal verbs with two particles have also
increased in recent years. The first of these two particles is
always an adverb. Phrasal verbs of this type likewise fall into
three categories: (1) The verb and the particles more or less
retain their separate meanings in *catch up on* or *with* (overtake,
get abreast of), *fall back on* (use as a reserve in the absence of
something better), *fall in with* (conform to, not stand out
against), *go through with* (finish), *look down on* (despise), *look
up to* (respect), *walk out on* (abandon). (2) The verb alone
retains its meaning in *cash in on* (profit from) originally used
in the card game of poker, *come in for* (receive), *go in for*
(practise), *live up to* (fulfil, especially an ideal or expectation).
(3) The constituents of this class show greater cohesion. The
speaker is seldom conscious of the significations of separate

words when he says *do away with* (abolish), *make up for* (compensate, recompense), *make up to* (court, fawn upon, try to be friends with), *put up with* (bear, tolerate, endure). *Get it over with*, an ellipsis of *get it over and done with*, which became fashionable in the sixties, has probably moved south from the north country.[1]

Phrasal verbs with two particles are described as redundant or pleonastic if they differ little in use and meaning from their simple forms: *check up on* for *check*, *face up to* for *face*, and *meet up with* for *meet*. From time to time protests are made against these in the correspondence columns of the daily press and elsewhere, but have the simpler forms exactly the same meanings? It might, for instance, be adduced in defence of *check up on* that *check* means 'test' in general. 'Check your tyres before the law does.'[2] 'Check and double check.' *Check up* (British) and *check on* (American) imply some kind of counting or computation, making sure that nothing is missing. *Check up on* implies yet closer examination and scrutiny. Scotland Yard detectives do not *check* but *check up on* a suspected criminal's past records and whereabouts. *Facing up to* a difficult situation means more than merely 'looking it in the face'. It means 'confronting' it (Lat. *frons, frontis* 'face, forehead'), 'meeting it with courage'. *Confrontation*, by the way, became an important vogue word in world power politics in the late sixties. *Meet up with* suggests fortuity. 'We met up with the Dean' implies that we encountered that officer quite by chance when we were least expecting to see him.

SUPPRESSED PREPOSITIONS

Side by side with this tendency to add redundant particles to verbs we detect the opposite trend to suppress them. *Agree*, like other intransitive verbs, is normally made transitive by the addition of a governing preposition. You normally *agree* (concur) *with* a person, *agree* (consent) *to* a measure, and *agree*

---

[1] See John Braine, *Room at the Top*, 1957, p. 206; James Kirkup, *Sorrows, Passions and Alarms*, 1959, p. 159.

[2] Stamped by the General Post Office on letters in the summer of 1968.

(decide) *on* a course of action by mutual consent. The first remains. You continue to agree or disagree with a person, but you can now talk of 'agreeing a plan' instead of 'agreeing to it' and of 'agreeing a policy' instead of 'agreeing on it'.

All the arrangements have been agreed
The Times 6 December 1965

New measures to defend the pound have been agreed by central bankers at Basle
The Times Business News 8 July 1968

Similarly you can now *approve* a plan, *compensate* a loss, and *protest* a wrong:

The Greater London Council approves a plan for car and pedestrian segregation in the West End, and compensates losses to property owners, but many stage-lovers protest the demolition of the Windmill Theatre
Summarized from the *Daily Telegraph* 10 July 1968

Instead of *belonging to* a place, you can now *belong* (cf. G *gehören*) absolutely; instead of *warning against*, you can *warn* (cf. G *warnen*) *that* + noun clause; and instead of *coping with* a difficult situation, you just *cope* or fail so to do.

It was easy to see that the new foreman did not belong
The Prime Minister warned that rebels would be penalized
Nurses are overworked and so tired that they can no longer cope
The Times 13 July 1968

Instead of 'Dream of a butterfly', DREAM A BUTTERFLY was the soothing slogan that greeted us from New York buses in 1967.

REVIVAL OF SUBJUNCTIVE FORMS

Apart from subjunctive *be* corresponding to indicative *am, are* and *is; were* to *was; have* to *has;* and *do* to *does;* no distinct subjunctive forms survive in standard speech. We are here, of course, concerned only with inherited forms and not with subjunctive substitutes involving the use of the modal auxiliaries *may, might, could, should* and *would*. Nevertheless, in literary writing the flexionless third person singular (with zero inflexion, as linguists sometimes say) resulting from the loss of OE -*e*, has an unbroken history down the ages. Now, especially in North America, it is being revived both in journalistic prose and in daily speech:

> It is necessary that he come without delay
> The directors have given instructions that the agent fly to Boston
> The judge insisted that the accused man appear in person
> I think it advisable that an armed guard stand in readiness

Has this revival any bearing on the future of English? Will the time come when our language, like Danish, has one unchanging form throughout the present tense? After all, our verbs have shed -*est* and -*eth* within living memory. In regional dialects in the United Kingdom, and in pidgin varieties in the Far East, flexionless *he go* instead of inflected *he goes* creates no difficulty in straightforward communication.

REDUCED FORMS

Reduced or contracted verbal forms are used more than ever today in both speech and writing. In describing them we find ourselves concerned once again with the anomalous finites.[1] *Have*, for instance, has its normal pronunciation [heiv] only in *be-have*. It has four other distinctive pronunciations [hav, həv, əv, v] according to emphasis, sentence position, whether the subject is a noun or a pronoun, and whether the preceding form ends in a vowel or a consonant.

Reduced Affirmative Forms

am	'm	I'm [aim]
is	's	he's, she's, it's, there's, where's, that's, what's, etc.

---

[1] To which we must now add *let's*. We are here concerned with words as forms and therefore it is more precise to say anomalous finites than auxiliaries, since this term relates to function.

are	're	we're, you're, they're
have	've	I've, you've, we've, they've
has	's	he's, she's, it's
had	'd	I'd, you'd, he'd, she'd, we'd, they'd
shall	'll	⎰ I'll, you'll, he'll, she'll, it'll
will	'll	⎱ we'll, they'll
would	'd	I'd, you'd, he'd, she'd, we'd, they'd
let us	let's	let's go, etc.

Reduced Negative Forms

Present	*Past*
I'm not (I aint [eint])	wasn't
isn't, aren't	wasn't, weren't
haven't, hasn't	hadn't
don't [dount], doesn't	didn't
shan't [ʃɑːnt]	shouldn't
won't [wount]	wouldn't
can't [kɑːnt]	couldn't
may not	mightn't
mustn't	
oughtn't to	
needn't	
daren't	usedn't to

When should one use these forms? Many teachers use reduced forms in their tape recordings, but full forms in their accompanying texts.[1] On the whole this would seem to be sound practice, but a growing number of technologists are now tacitly using reduced forms even in serious scientific writing in order to brighten up dull facts and (as they think) make closer contacts with their readers.

In speech the employment of reduced forms is being extended even at the highest levels. In writing, no longer excluded, it is left largely to the caprices of individual authors and printers. This important issue remains an open one.

[1] See the important article by Miss Myra Grech of the Australian National University at Canberra on 'Anomalous Finites and the Language Laboratory', *English Language Teaching* XXII (1967) 44–53.

CHAPTER 7

Changing Structures

WORD ORDER shows few changes and remains remarkably stable throughout the whole English-speaking community. Nevertheless, some interesting syntactic modifications are taking place within the main structures of sentences and to these we must now direct our attention.

LOSS OF THE DEFINITE ARTICLE

Some languages, like classical Latin and modern Russian, have no articles at all. Ancient Greek had a definite, but no indefinite article: modern Greek now has both. Old English, in its early West Saxon variety, had no articles, but it had demonstrative adjective-pronouns, one of which developed into an all-purpose *the* in Middle English. At the same time an indefinite article arose from the frequent use of the numeral *one*. In early Modern English the definite article was used more often than now. It was regularly used, for instance, with names of subjects of study and names of diseases and ailments. 'Angling may be said to be so like the mathematics,' wrote Izaak Walton, 'that it can never be fully learnt.'[1] Almost within living memory people spoke of 'the fever', 'the dropsy' and 'the measles'. 'Did you ever have the measles, and, if so, how many?'[2] John Earle, Professor of Anglo-Saxon at Oxford, invariably spoke of 'the *Beowulf*'. 'Madame Serena Merle turned away from the platform at the Euston Station,' wrote Henry James in 1881.[3] Today we drop the definite article before *university, campus* (but not

---

[1] *Compleat Angler*. Epistle to the Reader, 1653.
[2] Charles Farrar Browne (Artemus Ward), *The Census*, 1865.
[3] *The Portrait of a Lady*, Chapter xxxi.

precinct), *Government, press, radio, Bank Rate,* and many other expressions where it would have been obligatory a few years ago.

When the university was the only form of tertiary education in England, it was not regarded as an institution like school, college, church, chapel, synagogue, hospital or prison. Children went to school or college, worshippers to church, chapel or synagogue, sick folk to hospital, and malefactors to prison. But students went to the university. Before the year 1828 this could mean in England only to Oxford or Cambridge. When someone now observes that 'Mary goes to university (or starts at university) next October', this may still mean that she will go to Oxford or Cambridge, but in fact her choice of university may be decided for her by UCCA (University Central Council for Admissions) and she may eventually attend any one of those other institutions of learning which now hold tertiary status. On the face of it the omission of the article may appear to be something trivial, but in this instance it is significant. It marks a big change in the social life of England when 'going to university' becomes the right of every qualified teenager, even as 'going to school' has been compulsory for every normal child after the Forster Education Act of 1870.

It takes perhaps most students two semesters before they find their feet at university

The Listener 30 May 1968

Julian is only one of the three sons not to have gone to university

Sunday Times 21 July 1968

The government of the United States is referred to as the Administration. Do you regard the government of Britain as monolithic, or as one government among others? The custom is now being revived of referring to our two Houses as plain Government (with capitalization but without the article).

Britain is going for a long time yet to have a university system which relies heavily on financial support from Government

The Times 1 January 1966

There is talk of setting up some kind of an office staffed by
journalists to facilitate communication between press and
Government

The Times 3 August 1968

Have you noticed that the Bank Rate has recently become plain
Bank Rate? It corresponds to the Discount Rate in the United
States. Raising or reducing Bank Rate by only one per cent
affects a nation's whole economy. It is therefore unique. It is
no longer conceived as one definite rate among other rates of
the same kind, and so *the Bank Rate* becomes plain *Bank Rate*.

You may have noticed that the definite article is also being
tacitly dropped from the titles of books and periodicals. There
are, of course, three possibilities: definite article, indefinite
article, or zero. Between 1903 and 1913 Somerset Maugham
named three of his plays *The Tenth Man*, *A Man of Honour* and
Landed Gentry. Between 1937 and 1954 Noel Coward named
his three stints of autobiography *Present Indicative*, *Middle East
Diary* and *Future Indicative*, all three titles without articles. A
few years ago *The Radio Times* suddenly appeared as *Radio
Times* and *The New Statesman* became plain *New Statesman*.
More recently *The Spectator*, founded by Steele and Addison as
long ago as 1711, has become plain *Spectator*. In August 1959
The Manchester Guardian changed its title to *The Guardian*.
Will it appear one bright morning as simple *Guardian*?

Do you say *all the morning* or *all morning*, *all the day* or *all
day*, *all the winter* or *all winter*? The forms without articles, in
these and many other phrases, are certainly gaining ground.

COMPARISON OF ADJECTIVES

Another slight but interesting change is to be seen in the
growing use of *more* and *most* to express the comparative and
superlative degrees of adjectives instead of the endings *-er* and
-est. This change may be seen as another manifestation of that
trend from synthesis to analysis, or from complex to simple
forms, which has been going on for thousands of years in the

history of our language from Indo-European to modern English. It shows, in a very small way, that drift towards the invariable word which has proceeded to the very end in other languages like Chinese and Vietnamese. In the comparison of adjectives and adverbs, however, it is no more than a general drift. The old principles still hold. We still use *more* and *most* with adjectives of three syllables and more *(beautiful, more beautiful, most beautiful; adorable, more adorable, most adorable)*; we still add *-er* and *-est* to those of one syllable *(fine, finer, finest)*; and we still use both forms with adjectives of two syllables *(lovely, more lovely, most lovely* or *lovelier, loveliest)*. But today analytic forms with *more* and *most* (cf. F *plus beau, le plus beau*) are certainly increasing at the expense of synthetic forms in *-er* and *-est* (cf. G *schöner, schönst*). We hear people now say *more common* rather than *commoner, most pleasant* rather than *pleasantest*. We hear *more true* for *truer, more good* for *better*, even *more bad* for *worse*. Is this a passing fashion? 'I am the more bad', sighs Lavinia in L. P. Hartley's *Simonetta Perkins*, 'because I realize where my badness lies.' 'Wimbledon will be yet more hot tomorrow,' says the BBC news reader (1 July 1968). We sometimes hear people talking about 'facts that should be more well known' and 'the most well-dressed man in town' instead of 'better known' and 'best dressed'. These, you will agree, are innocuous in conversation, but hardly acceptable in careful writing. Meantime, as a move in the opposite direction, participles with *-est* terminations are not unknown: 'He's an American . . . thought London was on the way to being the leadingest place.' (John Osborne, *Time Present*.) 'The swingingest of all London clubs is in Park Lane' *(The Surrey Comet* 3 December 1966.) 'They have certainly done their damnedest [damdist]' *(The Times Literary Supplement* 22 August 1968).

We detect an interesting resuscitation of the demonstratives *this* and *that* as intensive adverbs:

Surely our statesmanship is not this bankrupt (= so bankrupt as all this, bankrupt to this degree)

The Times 20 January 1967

We do not often put together this many derivational suffixes
W. Nelson Francis, *The English Language* 1967, p. 35

The voyage from Montreal to New York is not all that
simple (= not quite so simple as all that)
The Listener 7 September 1967

PERSONAL PRONOUNS

By definition pronouns are not lexical words or words of full
meaning. They are grammatical words, structure words or
functors, and in most languages there have been periods of time
when pronouns have undergone changes. We are now witnessing such a time in the history of English, but we are fortunate
in having to deal with no great multiplicity of forms. After all,
if we parade all the personal pronouns and their possessive
adjectives in one table, we find that they come to only twenty-
three.

Subjective	Objective	Possessive Adjective	Possessive Pronoun
I	me	my	mine
we	us	our	ours
you		your	yours
he	him	his	
she	her		hers
it		its	
they	them	their	theirs

The forms of the so-called second person, or person addressed,
have suffered five regrettable losses: all four forms *thou*, *thee*,
thy and *thine* in the singular, and subjective *ye* in the plural.

'Lovest thou me?' in the King James Bible becomes 'Do you love me?' in the New English Bible (John xxi 16). 'Ye in me' becomes 'You in me' (John xiv 20). That loss has been a substantial one in those situations where it may be requisite to distinguish between one person addressed and more than one. In such situations the speaker may feel himself obliged to say 'you all;[1] yes, all of you; every one of you, as many as are here present; you people, you fellows, you guys, you men and women, you ladies, you gentlemen, you boys, you girls'; or, against his better judgement, he is compelled to say youse [ju:z], unstressed [jəz].[2] If you look once again at this table of personal pronouns you will observe that only five of the seven have distinctive forms for subjective and objective (*I:me we:us he:him she:her* and *they:them*). These, and these alone, constitute those notorious 'disputed areas' over which verbal battles are still fought. Clearly the time has come for us to recognize that objective forms are gradually superseding subjective ones (a) as complements of the substantive verb (*It's me* side by side with *It is I*), and (b) as emphatic isolates (*Them and us* side by side with *They and we*). That is all. In both instances the choice is a binary one, depending upon speech register and situational context.

It is I retains its rightful place in serious discourse (Lat. *sum ego*, OE *hit eom ic*, ME *It am I*). It's me, with *it is* suitably reduced to *it's*, stands as its conversational counterpart. Notice, by the way, that *it* is here discriminative, as in T. S. Eliot's *The Elder Statesman*: 'It's not you and me he rejects' = It is not you and I that he rejects (but someone else).[3]

[1] In OED First Supplement (1933) *you-all* is marked U.S. and the first instance given is from Henry Louis Mencken, *The American Language* 1919, p. 215: 'In the South . . . the true plural is commonly indicated by you-all'.

[2] Designated *substandard* by Webster III and *nonstandard* by RHD. In EDD *yous* is assigned to 'Ireland, America, Australia. Also in forms *youse* (America, Australia) and *youz* (Donegal)'. The earliest quotation in EDD comes from T. C. Croker, *Fairy Legends and Traditions of South Ireland* 1862, p. 201: 'Youz live to a powerful age here under the water'.

[3] Cf. expletive *it* in 'It is raining', and anticipatory *it* in 'It is the pace that kills'.

The feeling is strong that a verb, even the verb *to be*, should be followed by the objective case:

> *Be thou, Spirit fierce,*
> *My spirit. Be thou me, impetuous one*
> Shelley, *Ode to the West Wind*

> Heedless of grammar, they all cried, 'That's him'
> Barham, *The Jackdaw of Rheims*

> I am she, she me, till death and beyond it
> George Meredith, *The Egoist*

> And let us remember that, but for him, there might have been no Wanstead and Woodford, no us, and no Britain
> Field Marshal Viscount Montgomery of Alamein speaking at the unveiling of the statue of Sir Winston Churchill at Woodford, 31 October 1959

> There were only three regular correspondents left: the *New York Times*, the Associated Press (another American) and me from the BBC
> René Cutforth in *The Listener* 30 August 1968

The third chapter of Richard Hoggart's *The Uses of Literacy* (1957) is entitled *'Them' and 'Us'*. 'Them' are the people who are 'not us', that is, not the working class, who toil daily. 'Them' are Government, the local authority, the law, the police, the officials, who do no productive work. 'Them' are not altogether evil, but, because 'not us', they must be watched, suspected, opposed. To change the title of this sociological study of class consciousness to grammatical *They and We* would obviously spoil everything.

In July 1968 a television play bore the title *It's Only Us*, and on 10 August in the same year a comedy film was broadcast under the announced title *He and She* – 'or better,' added the announcer, speaking on the spur of the moment, *Him and Her*. By 'better' he meant 'more avant-garde', but he probably missed the point. He failed to realize that this series of comedy films was intended by its author to be not slapstick lowbrow *Him and Her*, but refined and sophisticated *He and She*. To

sum up, we now recognize two cases of pronouns corresponding
to two levels of discourse:

(a)	It is I	It's me
	That is he	That's him
	These are they	They're them
(b)	You and I	Me and you
	He and she	Him and her
	They and we	Them and us

WHO OR WHOM

No one, however, ever says *who's whom*, the personal counterpart of *what's what* and *which is which*. *Who's Who* happens to be
the title of an annual biographical dictionary of contemporary
men and women, first issued in 1849.[1] *Who was Who*, the title
of the volumes collecting decades of completed life-histories
(Volume I 1897–1915), goes back to Chaucer.[2]

Nearly half a century ago Edward Sapir (in *Language*, pp.
166–74) predicted the demise of *whom*, showing at great length
that it was doomed because it was 'psychologically isolated'
from the objective pronouns *me, us, him, her, them* on the one
hand, and the invariables *which, what, that* and *where, when, how,
why* on the other. Does Sapir's prediction now show signs of
being fulfilled? The answer is no, not yet. In interrogative
sentences *whom* immediately following a preposition shows no

---

[1] It is interesting to note that M. André Siegfried could not bring
himself to stretch a point and say *Qui est?* or *Qui est Qui?* in French.
He therefore chose *Who's Who in France* as his title. 'L'expression
Who's Who est difficile à traduire et c'est pourquoi on l'a conservée ici
comme disant bien, en fin de compte, ce qu'elle veut dire.' Its French
rival, which is more selective, bears the somewhat cumbersome title
Dictionnaire Biographique Français Contemporain. Its Belgian counterpart
is called more simply *Le Livre Bleu*.

[2] Symkyn the miller's wife could not distinguish individuals in that
moonlit bedroom at Trumpington –

> *And by that light she saugh hem bothe two*
> *But sikerly she nyste who was who*
>
> *The Reeve's Tale* 380

sign of weakening. We still like to have two ways of saying a
thing:

> To whom did you give it?
> Who did you give it to?
> Of whom were you thinking?
> Who were you thinking of?
>
> For whom is this book intended?
> Who is this book intended for?

So also in relative clauses, where we have no end preposition
alternatives, we have no choice but to retain whom:

> These are the classes of people between whom disputes are
> likely to arise
> He is not a man from whom truth can be withheld indefinitely
> His parents, from whom he inherited considerable gifts, both
> died young

Strange as it may seem, we occasionally encounter *who's* for
whose:

> The prosecution made a detailed analysis of the disturbance:
> who hit whom, who stepped on who's foot
>
> *The Times* 28 December 1967

ORDER OF ATTRIBUTIVE ADJECTIVES

The general tightening of word sequence leaves French-derived
nominal phrases like *court martial*, *Chapel Royal*, and *tiger proper*
intact since these are used in special registers, whether legal,
or ecclesiastical, or heraldic. So *Attorney General*, *Lords Spiritual*
and *Temporal*, *notary public*, *heir apparent*, *heir presumptive*,
County Palatine, *body politic*, *freehold absolute*, *proof positive*,
malice prepense (beside *malice aforethought* with second component English); *Church Militant*, *Vicar Apostolic*, *light perpetual*,
the life immortal (Advent Collect); *Mount Pleasant* (nickname
for a London refuse heap), *Siege Perilous* (Arthurian Romance),
Palace Beautiful (Bunyan), *in order serviceable* (Milton), *Castle
Dangerous* (Scott), and very many more. The postposed epithet

sometimes endows an expression with an indefinable affectiveness. This is one of the miracles of language. Why does it mean so much to say that a custom has been observed *from time immemorial?* It merely infers that that custom is older than any living man can remember. Why, I ask (but cannot answer) does 'the vision splendid' of Wordsworth's *Intimations of Immortality*, expressing, as it does, all the bright unsullied aspirations of youth, signify so very much more than 'the splendid vision'?

> *The youth, who daily farther from the east*
> *Must travel, still is Nature's priest,*
> *And by the vision splendid*
> *Is on his way attended;*
> *At length the man perceives it die away,*
> *And fade into the light of common day.*

It would indeed be illuminating to survey the long history of our poetic inheritance with an eye to these postposed attributives alone.

In heraldry a *peacock proper* denotes not a symbolic creature, but a picture of a living bird in its natural colouring. *Proper*, by the way, is the only adjective surviving (as against many in French) which has a different meaning when postposed. Compare 'proper behaviour' with 'architecture proper'. In the sense 'strictly so called, in the precise signification of the term' postposed *proper* remains in general use. For instance, 'the Port of London proper' means the ninety navigable miles of the River Thames controlled by PLA (the Port of London Authority) from the Nore Estuary upstream to Teddington Weir, neither more nor less.

Adjectives may be classed as attributive, as in 'The white house stands on a hill'; predicative, as in 'The house is white' or 'John has painted his house white'; and appositive, as in 'White and gleaming, the house dominates the hillside'. All three functional types are very much alive. One of the more interesting features of current usage is the growing tendency on the part of 'the folk' to feel their way towards an established sequence in the arrangement of multiple epithets.

In 1960 London Transport displayed a notice at Golders Green Station reminding visitors to 'go and see the house where Keats heard the nightingale and spent his brilliant five short creative years'. They were the years from 1816 to 1821, from sonnet to sonnet, from 'On First Looking into Chapman's Homer' to 'Bright Star, would I were stedfast as thou art!' The notice was both attractive and effective. It prompted more than one casual observer to step out smartly in the direction of Keats Grove, but what can be deduced from the order of the constituents of that multiple attribution? Clearly *creative years* cohere: all too short, those five years were 'brilliantly creative' rather than 'creatively brilliant'.[1] But let us look a little more closely at those other epithets. Should not the quantifier *five* come between the determiner *his* and the general qualifier *short?* Try saying

'his five short brilliant creative years'.

The order of attributives, it would seem, is gradually settling down. It is determined partly by custom. Cohesion is analysable in terms of immediate, mediate, and ultimate constituents. Attributes expressing permanent qualities stand nearest the head-noun: 'long white beard', 'tall standard roses', 'six-lane elevated freeway'. It is surely only from custom that we say 'strong silent man' and not 'silent strong man', 'great big elephant' and not 'big great elephant', 'sweet young thing' and not 'young sweet thing'. From custom we place contrasting antonyms after the noun they modify:

times good and bad
places near and far
ways fair and foul
streets wide and narrow
love sacred and profane
hymns ancient and modern (Baker)
English past and present (Trench)
plays pleasant and unpleasant (Shaw)

[1] *Creative* was a vogue word in the fifties. Writers of school textbooks claimed to teach not plain *English* but *Creative English,* and literary critics sought to evoke in their readers not *appreciative response* but *creative response.*

From custom we put colour and material after size and shape: 'my little white house', 'that long wooden shed'. But is the colour of my house really more permanent than its size? Perhaps I will have it painted green next spring. It will be more difficult, not to say expensive, to have it enlarged. Such considerations, of course, do not count in language. The point is that colour is more closely linked with the object than size is in the consciousness of the speaker. It is the mental picture that decides linguistic expression, not objective reality. Witness numerous western placenames embodying a component signifying 'white': Whitby, Whitchurch, Whitchester; Weissenburg, Weissenstadt; Bilovec, Belogradchik; Casablanca, Villalba, and scores of others.

Along these lines, then, we venture to set up the following model for the order of constituents in multiple attribution:

1 determiner
2 quantifier (often a cardinal numeral)
3 adjective of quality (generally descriptive)
4 adjective of size, shape, or texture
5 adjective of colour or material
6 noun adjunct (if any)
7 head-noun

Here are half a dozen nominal groups in which the model may be seen to work fairly well:

1	2	3	4	5	6	7
a	dozen		large	red	Spalding	tulips
that	one	solid	round	oak	dining	table
	many	fine	tall	brown	beech	hedges
	several	nice	little	brick	Tudor	cottages
some	twenty	trim		black	race	horses
those	countless	unforget-table	long	bright	summer	evenings

You may feel that these phrases sound somewhat artificial and you are doubtless justified, but the important thing to notice is that most people, not only in south-east England but throughout the whole English-speaking world, would put their attributives in that order, quite naturally, without even thinking about it.

The fact that *preposition* means 'before placing' (Lat. *prae-positio* translating Gk *pro-thesis*) has undoubtedly helped to create the notion that this relation-word should stand before the word it governs, not after it, and certainly not at the very end of a sentence. And yet we find good postpositions throughout our entire history and we favour them more and more in current English.

> John slept the clock round
> This is known all the world over
> Why not live all the year round in comfort?
> We searched the whole place through and found no trace

Much depends, we may say, upon our habitat and environment, or the place in which we live
> which we live in
> that we live in
> where we live
> we live in

Of these five relative or attributive clauses, all grammatically acceptable, the last two are now the most frequently used. In succinctness and brevity there is nothing to choose between these last two, but most people now, I think, would prefer the rhythm of the last one of all.

> the pláce where we líve
> the pláce we líve in

Compare:
> We have been gathering bilberries, but we have brought
>> nothing in which to put them
>> nothing to put them in
> Here we have a tin of lovely peaches, but unfortunately we have nothing with which to open it
>> nothing to open it with

The second alternative is now current in both instances.

Prepositions may now have more uses than one:

The wreck was seen by the seashore (place)
  by the coastguard (agent)

The picture was painted by a new technique (instrument)
  by a competent artist (agent)

The judge was utterly exhausted by a prolonged session (cause)
  by midnight (time)

Ambiguities may sometimes arise:
The car was stopped by the wall
may mean

   (a) The wall stopped the car
or (b) John stopped the car near the wall

Prepositions are seldom static. They enlarge or reduce their areas of relationship. Nowhere is this better seen than in the Slavonic languages. Starting from Prague and moving north-eastwards through Poland and White Russia to Moscow, you can observe prepositions changing kaleidoscopically, gradually, almost imperceptibly. And so it has been in our own history in time, rather than in space. Starting from Old English, you can take any preposition like *after* or *of* and observe gradual changes down the ages. Today *about* is encroaching on *of*. We still say 'Talk of the devil, and he is sure to appear' because it is a popular proverb. It is found on the very first page of Swift's *Polite Conversation*, showing that it goes back to the eighteenth century at least. We still say 'nothing to speak *of*', an inherited phrase, but 'nothing to write home *about*', a more recent cliché. Do you say 'ignorant of' or 'ignorant about'? Both James Hilton in *And Now Good-bye* (1931) and Nevil Shute in *Requiem for a Wren* (1955) use the latter, although no reputable dictionary records it.[1]

---

[1] Sverker Brorström, *The Increasing Frequency of the Preposition About.* Stockholm Studies in English IX, 1963.

Undoubtedly *about* is enlarging its area of use:

> We did not expect what happened and we are very disappointed about it
>
> *The Sunday Times* 4 August 1968

> Nurses were most concerned about patient care (= with the care of their patients)
>
> *The Times* 16 August 1968

So, too, is *on:*

> We need have no fears on the future of technical education (= fears for the future)

> They argued for hours on the rights and wrongs of equal pay (= argued over the rights)

This increase in the uses of *about* and *on* is to be warmly welcomed if it makes for brevity and clarity, and if it leads to a diminution in the employment of cumbrous phrases like *in connexion with, in reference to, with regard to, in respect of, in the case of, in the matter of,* and many more.

MOBILE ADVERBS

Let us imagine that a witness has just stated publicly that 'the man was living a double life' and that he now suddenly realizes that he has gone too far. He decides to soften his statement down a little. Was the fellow a schizophrenic like Dr Jekyll and Mr Hyde? Was he running two homes? Or was he a secret agent? The witness may salve his conscience by saying (a) 'Apparently the man was living a double life'; (b) 'The man apparently was living a double life'; (c) 'The man was apparently living a double life'; (d) 'The man was living apparently a double life'; or (e) 'The man was living a double life apparently'. In (a) the adverb is said to be *attitudinal:* it modifies the whole statement, and not just one part of it. Its initial position gives it emphasis and it is followed by single-bar juncture which may be indicated in writing by a comma. Stress and tone change in (b) and, according to context, they might very well change in such a way as to imply 'the man and not the woman'. In (c) the meaning is much the same as in (a) but the modifying adverb, occupying its normal position between auxiliary and verb, is less attitudinal and less emphatic. In (d) the adverb is less emphatic still. It is a very gentle downtoner. It is almost parenthetical and it might even be placed within commas accordingly. In (e) it is added as a kind of afterthought and it bears weak stress. Nevertheless, it could have considerable legal significance if it were said in such a way as to imply that conclusive evidence was not forthcoming.

In this brief sentence, then, all five positions are possible. Since adverbs are incidental components and are indeed less essential than any other parts of speech, they are on that account more mobile than any others. Nevertheless, the general tendency to make word order more fixed in present-day English applies, though in a lesser degree, to adverbs also.

Adverbs of frequency usually stand after the substantive verb ('They are seldom late'), before other verbs ('You never know'), and between an auxiliary and its full verb ('You can never tell').[1]

Adverbs of time usually stand at the beginning or end of a sentence, seldom in the middle. Particular expressions of time precede more general ones: 'Adolf Hitler died at half past three in the afternoon on the last day of April in the year 1945'. An adverb of place or direction follows the verb with which it is bound semantically: 'We arrived home at seven'. Other adverbs normally take end positions in the order of manner, place and time: 'The Home Secretary spoke at great length in the House last night.' Sentences introduced by *there* stand apart because this adverb serves as a blank or dummy subject. The substantive verb never stands first in a statement. If, for instance, the host discovers one chair short at a party just as the guests are taking their places at table, he cannot say (as in many other languages) 'Is a chair in the study' or even 'A

---

[1] But after the auxiliary ('You never can tell') in General American. In his play of that name (1898) Shaw followed transatlantic usage. 'Man is the only creative animal on earth, though paradoxically his resistance to change sometimes can be almost heroically obstinate'.
Robert Strange McNamara, *The Essence of Security*, 1968.

chair is in the study', but 'There's a chair' or 'You will find an extra chair in the study'.

POSITIVE TAGS AS AFTERTHOUGHTS

In our survey of anomalous finites (p. 126) we have seen that negative tags follow positive statements, and vice versa:

> We all agree on this, don't we?
> We don't disagree on this, do we?

In recent years a new type of interrogative phrase has become fashionable in which a positive tag (often introduced by *or* or *but*) follows a positive statement:

> We all agree on this, or do we?

I first heard it in 1952 and I thought it very effective. Added after a slight pause, it calls upon the hearer or reader to think again, to rouse himself from mental complacency, and to re-examine the validity of an affirmation too readily accepted. This positive appendage has its own peculiar rhythm and intonation:

> These are the fruits of our labours over a period of thirty years, or are they?
> We know in our hearts that we shall be rewarded, or do we?
> The proceeds from the national lottery would be applied to meritorious purposes like medical research, sports stadiums, and grand opera. But would they?
>
> *The Times* 29 June 1968

> Long lazy summer days are made for nurses to enjoy. Or are they?
>
> *The Times* 25 July 1968

> The Roman Emperor Titus took the Menorah when he destroyed the Temple in A.D. 70. Or did he? Was it perhaps a copy?
>
> *Penguin Book News* September 1968

ELLIPSES OLD AND NEW

An ellipsis sometimes remains so long in common use that the original full form may recede into oblivion. The date 1 May 1970[1] is not so much a contraction as an ellipsis of 'The first day of the month of May in the year of grace nineteen seventy'. *Five o'clock* stands for 'five hours of the clock' contrasted with five hours' duration. *Of course* is short for 'as a matter of course'; *above all* for 'above all things', older 'above all thing', with neuter plural zero inflexion maintained far into the eighteenth century; *good morning* for 'God give you a good morning'; and *as green as green* for 'as green as green can ever be'. To *execute* a felon means 'to execute the sentence of the court' passed upon him. To *make ends meet* is better than *make both ends meet* since it signifies 'to make ends of the balance account of the year meet even'. *Easier said than done* sounds ungrammatical only if you forget its expanded form 'easier when said than when done'. *Well I never!* is an ancient aposiopesis – 'Well I never did hear anything like that before'. To *stay put* implies 'to stay where you have been put'. *This, that and what not* means 'this, that, and whatever is not included under *this* and *that*'.

Be seeing you, short for 'I'll be seeing you again soon', became fashionable among teenagers in the late thirties. It implied a temporary farewell as compared with the more permanent *adieu* [əˈdjuː] and *goodbye*. Presumably (I cannot prove it) it was an infiltration into youthful speech of the European 'to the seeing again' type of leavetaking (F *au revoir*, G *auf Wiedersehen*, Ital. *arrivederci*, Russ. *do svidanija*). Compared with the slightly older *See you soon*, it showed that growing preference for the progressive present which we were discussing in the previous chapter.

---

[1] This is now the accepted form in Britain – day, month, year – unpunctuated and unabbreviated.

F

CHAPTER 8

Functional Shifts

I<small>T</small> I<small>S</small> because word order is more fixed than ever before that functional shifts within sentence structures are made feasible without jeopardizing intelligibility. One part of speech operates as some other part of speech. Old words rejuvenesce. Speech is suddenly endowed with a fresh vitality, variety and power.

Form, function and *meaning* – that useful linguistic triad – may be simply defined as follows. *Form* is primarily phonemic: /ai/ the person speaking, /nau/ the passing moment. *Function* denotes the work done by a form within a tagmemic pattern. *Meaning* is fundamentally referential – the relationship, or series of relationships, between form, or forms, and reality.

The ordering of forms into word-classes or parts of speech is arbitrary, with one important exception in Indo-European, namely, the verb. The verb is *verbum 'the* word'. In any system of word-classes, however wildly experimental, it always stands alone. The interjection, a mere noise 'thrown between' – *ah! bah! hélas!* – stands outside: it is not really a part of speech at all. We can, if we wish, arrange the remaining six parts of speech in two neat triads:

noun, pronoun, adjective (nominals)
adverb, preposition, conjunction (particles).

We have already discussed the nominals in the first of these triads in Chapter 5. By calling the members of the second triad *particles*, we cover the (only slightly) diverse functions performed by *after* in the three statements

John came after (adverb)
John came after me (preposition)
John came after I did (conjunction).

There is much to be said for making determiners (definite and indefinite articles, demonstrative pronouns, some, any, etc.) and cardinal numerals (one, two, three, etc.) separate parts of speech. If we do this, we then have verbs, three nominals, three particles, determiners and numerals as our nine word-classes. We then have just as many parts of speech as there were muses in Greek mythology and spheres in Dante's universe.

Every sentence is a frame into which syntactic units, or tagmemes, are fitted. When a word is forced into an unusual tagmemic slot, it is said to undergo *grammatical conversion* or *functional shift*. For instance, when Enobarbus is eagerly explaining (in *Antony and Cleopatra* II ii 191) to Agrippa in Rome exactly what Cleopatra looked like as she glided along the river of Cydnus in all her glory, he said that she 'beggared', not 'impoverished', all description.

> *I will tell you*
> *The barge she sat in, like a burnish'd throne,*
> *Burn'd on the water . . . For her own person,*
> *It beggar'd all description; she did lie*
> *In her pavilion, cloth-of-gold of tissue,*
> *O'erpicturing that Venus where we see*
> *The fancy outwork nature.*

The earliest instance of *beggar* as a verb is recorded in the OED for the year 1528. To *beggar description* means 'to make all description seem poor in comparison with the reality'. Shakespeare here gives this verb the inflexion of the past tense. Because the new verb fits naturally into an accepted structural frame, there is not the slightest danger of ambiguity. After the lapse of nearly four centuries people still talk about something 'beggaring description' if they think it so lovely that 'words fail them' to describe it.

This is not the place to go into the history of English syntax, but it is profitable to take a quick look here and now at some quite simple sentence frames. We shall find two main patterns with five subsidiary structures within each. Verb and complement together comprise the predicate. (*Complement* is here used as a comprehensive term to cover both *complement* and *object* as used by traditional grammarians.)

SIMPLE SENTENCE FRAMES

First Pattern

	Subject	Verb	Complement
1	A cat	has	nine lives
	Every dog	has	his day
	All the world	loves	a lover
	The good	will overcome	the evil
	The hungry	have found	food
2	Science	is	organized knowledge
	A good example	is	the best sermon
	Seeing	is	believing
	To work	is	to pray
	To love her	is	a liberal education
3	Elizabeth	became	queen
	The crofter's grandson	rose to be	prime minister
	The club secretary	was elected	president
	This lowly man	happened to be	a famous surgeon
	The miner's daughter	grew up	a lovely woman
4	Food	was running	short
	The shipwrecked crew	landed	safe and sound
	The captain	fell	sick
	The accident	proved	fatal
	Both men	pleaded	guilty
5	Truth	lay	hidden
	Nothing	passed	unobserved
	The village	appeared	deserted
	The backroom boys	worked	unseen
	John's worst fears	proved	unfounded

You will observe that the complement in (1) is the direct object of a transitive verb; in (2) it is a predicative noun forming the second constituent of an equation linked to the first by the meaningless copula *is*; in (3) it is also a predicative noun linked with the subject by various meaningful verbs and verbal groups; in (4) it is a predicative adjective; whereas in (5) it is a predicative past participle.

Second Pattern

Sentences of the second pattern contain four components: subject, verb, and two complements, first and second, or inner and outer.

	Subject	Verb	Inner Complement	Outer Complement
6	John	gave	Mary	a ring
	The players	stood	one another	drinks
	The chairman	offered	him	the job
	I	bought	my wife	a stole
	That	will teach	him	a lesson
7	Pope Leo	crowned	Charlemagne	emperor
	The pupils	called	their teacher	names
	An innate nobility	made	him	a leader
	The crew	chose	him	captain
	Historians	consider	Marlborough	a peerless general
8	The sailors	painted	the town	red
	I	like	my coffee	strong
	That	drove	him	mad
	The children	made	their mother	angry
	We	feel	ourselves	unworthy
9	Everyone	thought	the cause	ruined
	We	could not make	ourselves	understood
	The driver	found	the road	flooded
	I	regard	the matter	closed
	The President	wanted	the prisoners	released

10 This	would have made	a cat	laugh
We	heard	them	groan
I	want	you all	to know
They	told	him	to go
The coroner	ordered	the letter	to be opened

You will observe that the inner and outer complements in (6) consist of indirect object (without preposition) followed by direct object; in (7) these complements are direct object and appositive noun; in (8) direct object and predicative adjective; in (9) direct object and predicative past participle; and in (10) direct object and predicative infinitive. You will also notice that in all these fifty simple declarative sentences you can seldom change the word order without at the same time doing something else – adding, subtracting something, or changing the meaning. There is no better way of appreciating the importance of word order in present-day English than by scrutinizing these fifty sentences. For instance, in the first sentence of (6) you might well add 'to' and say 'John gave a ring to Mary' but not 'John gave a ring Mary'. Why not? Because people hold it in memory that prepositionless indirect objects constitute inner complements. In other words, our inherited framework requires that an indirect object comes first when *to* is omitted. Certain verbs, like *explain* and *say*, never leave out *to*. 'My father explained the details to me.' 'He said these things to me.' In the second sentence of (8) you might omit *my* and say 'I like strong coffee', but this would obviously be a more general statement about my predilection for strong coffee, whereas, as it stands, 'I like my coffee strong' could be a quite particular statement and even a veiled instruction to someone about to make coffee. In the third sentence of (10) you might say 'I want to know you all' with a complete change in meaning. In the last sentence but one 'Him they told to go' would show shift of emphasis, implying that they allowed others to stay.

PARTIAL CONVERSION

Let us now return for a moment to the last two sentences in (1).

The good is the good thing, or all that is good in the world (G *das Gute*). *The good* or plain *good* (with or without the article) is adjective functioning as noun. *The hungry*, on the other hand, are human beings who are hungry (and here the article is obligatory), hungry people (G *die Hungrigen*). *The hungry* shows an adjective functioning as a noun with a difference of meaning. These shifts might be both labelled *partial conversions*.[1]

Conversions become complete when the resultant forms assume plural inflexions:
the undesirables = people or things not wanted
the imponderables = factors that cannot be accurately weighed or estimated.

So also: countables, uncountables (in grammar);
variables, constants (in mathematics);
eatables, drinkables, necessaries, valuables.
The plural inflexion has long been extended to present participles:

offerings, rejoicings, sighings, sorrowings, shortcomings.

It is now being extended to a limited number of past participles:

the retireds = old people who have retired from active work, now sometimes called euphemistically 'senior citizens'
the unwanteds = people (especially children) who are not wanted by society
the young marrieds = people who have married young
the newly weds = the recently wedded ones
the coloureds = formerly non-whites in general, but now generally taken to mean 'of mixed blood, not wholly of white descent'.

MULTIPLE CONVERSION

A word may shift its function more than once. Take, for example, the form *down* meaning 'hill' as in North and South Downs, those two ranges of chalk hills stretching from east to west in the counties of Kent, Surrey and Sussex in south-east

[1] First so named by Henry Sweet in *A New English Grammar Logical and Historical*, Part I, 1891, § 107.

England. 'My parents,' I may say, 'now live on the North Downs.' From the phrase *of down*, OE *of dune* 'from the hill' comes the adverb *adown*, later *down*, as in the sentence 'Two trees fell down in the gale'. From adverb to preposition the transition is easy: 'The stream tumbled down the slope'. From adverb or preposition to attributive adjective, however, the shift is far more functional: 'Let us all meet on the down platform.' We are at once understood because no other part of speech than an adjective can possibly stand between *the* and *platform* in this particular sentence frame. If we then speak of workmen going on strike and *downing* tools, or going to the village inn and *downing* their mugs of ale, we are clearly using *down* as a verb. Finally, if we find a friend in the doldrums, and if we gently remind him that 'we all have our *ups* and *downs*', the wheel of transition has come full circle, and *down* functions as a noun once more.

To sum up, we find the word *down* performing the following different functions in current speech:

My parents now live on the North Downs (noun)
Two trees fell down in the gale (adverb)
The stream tumbled down the slope (preposition)
Let us all meet on the down platform (adjective)
The workmen downed their mugs of ale (verb)
We all have our ups and downs (noun again)

NOUNS INTO VERBS

Today the commonest conversions are from nouns into verbs and from verbs into nouns. In Chinese and Malay these interchanges are intrinsic and universal since in those languages nouns and verbs are one. In Indo-European languages, apart from rare exceptions in Scandinavian, such interchanges are made possible only by the use of affixes. Straight conversions are easy in modern English because, having lost their inflexions, many nouns and verbs are identical; especially monosyllabic forms like *deal, hate, hope, hold, fight, leap, love, step*, and many more. Which came first, noun or verb, can nearly always be ascertained by consulting the Oxford English Dictionary. In many cases common sense will decide. *Head*, for instance, was initially a substantive. It was first used as a verb in *Cursor Mundi* (1300) just like G *köpfen* 'to behead'. Heading the ball in Association Football is not mentioned before 1897. We first encounter the verb *finger* 'to play upon an instrument with the fingers' in Barclay's *Eclogues* (1515): 'Yet could he pipe and finger well a drone'. In its present sense 'to touch or turn about in one's fingers' it appeared in Spenser's *Faerie Queene*, Book iii (1589): 'To finger the fine needle and nyce thread'. We first encounter the verb *face* 'to show a bold face, look big' in the fifteenth century. Names of many other parts of the human body – *eye, nose, mouth, arm, breast, shoulder, elbow, hand, knuckle, thumb, stomach, leg, foot, heel* and *toe* – have come to be used as verbs. Before looking them up in the OED, you will, of course, make an independent guess on your own account. (Surmise before consulting: after consulting verify.) You will find that the Earl of Kent (in *King Lear* IV iii 44) uses *elbow* as a verb in the sense 'to jostle': 'A sovereign shame so elbows him'. You will find that the boatswain (in *The Tempest* I i 20) uses *hand* as a verb in the sense 'to handle' when he says to that honest old counsellor Gonzalo: 'If you can command these elements to silence, and work the peace of the present, we will not hand a rope more'. You will be surprised to discover that *toe a line* is first recorded in Captain Frederick Marryat's *Peter Simple* of 1833; 'He desired us to toe a line, which means to stand in a row'. In political parlance *toeing the line* or 'conforming to defined party standards' is now in daily use.

Has the time come when any noun can be made to function as a verb? We should here distinguish, I think, between permanent shifts that reflect changes in social habit and way of life, and temporary shifts that are made by speakers and writers in quest of stylistic novelty. To the first class belong such expressions as to *audition* (a candidate for an appointment in show business), to *garage* (a car), to *headline* (an item of news), to *pinpoint* (a problem or a defect), to *process*[1] (articles of food), to *radio* (a

[1] Distinguish between *process* 'to subject food or material to some special treatment', noun-into-verb shift (1884) and *pro'cess* 'to walk in procession' backformation after *aggress, progress, transgress*, etc. (1814).

message), and to *service* (a car, computer, or automatic machine). To the second class belong such expressions as to *rubbish Mr Smith* 'to assert persistently that whatever Mr Smith says or writes is rubbish', and to *host a luncheon* 'to act as host at a luncheon party'.

It was Robert Ackley, this guy that *roomed* right next to me
J. D. Salinger, *The Catcher in the Rye*, 1951, p. 25

The car moved west . . . till it reached Madison Avenue, and then it *rightangled* sharply north
J. D. Salinger, *Raise High the Roof Beam, Carpenters*,
1955, p. 31

The classes in this university were not of the kind you could *breeze into* unannounced
The Listener 29 February 1968

Ex-General Salan might be *amnestied*
Sunday Times 9 June 1968

The deputies at the Chicago Conference felt that they were being *railroaded* into accepting a compromise
Radio 4 28 August 1968

Some American and Australian shifts like 'to *author* a book on trade relations', 'to *pressure* a company director to cut dividends', and 'to *position* a factory near a turnpike' meet with little approval in Britain. Why not say *write, force* and *place*?

VERBS INTO NOUNS

A verb may shift into a noun more than once in its history. *Break*, for instance, denoted 'act of breaking' as early as 1300: 'wit-vten brek of ani bogh' in *Cursor Mundi*. It was not used in the sense of 'interval' until 1689. *Dig*, denoting a tool for digging, is documented as early as 1674, but in the sense 'act of digging, archaeological excavation' it did not occur until 1887. *Drive*, denoting 'act of driving' is also recorded as early as

1697, but in the sense 'carriage road' it first appeared in Maurice Keatinge's *Travels through France and Spain to Morocco* of 1816. This is noteworthy in view of the fact that over thirty roads in Greater London are named *The Drive* and thousands of other roads are called *Drives* with modifying epithets in London and various parts of England. Some eight London roads are called *The Rise*, but the noun *rise*, when it was first used in 1410, figured as a hunting term. Thomas Fuller employed it in its present sense in his *Holy War* of 1639: 'The Jews were forbidden to enter into Jerusalem or so much as to behold it from any rise or advantage of ground'. Today *mix* for *mixture* and *capsize* for *capsizing* are characteristically recent shifts:

Khrushchev's political power is viewed as being at no time a definite quantum, but rather an unstable *mix* of his native political skills and his accumulated prestige
Carl A. Linden, *Khrushchev and the Soviet Leadership*, 1967

At present we have too few people with this kind of skill *mix*
F. R. Jevons in *The Listener* 11 May 1967

Three children were lost in a boat *capsize*
The Times 29 April 1967

No less characteristically recent are *construct*, *transform* and *transplant* which are partly (a) verb-into-noun shifts of the type we have just been considering, and (b) convenient contractions of the nouns in -*(a)tion*: *construction*, *transformation* and *transplantation*. When, in 1965, the first successful cardiac swop was achieved in South Africa, it was described indifferently as a *transplantation* or a *transplant*. A few years later, when spare-part surgery was taking leaps ahead in various parts of the world, *transplantation* was already outmoded. Everyone talked about *heart transplants*.

Among the commonest of recent shifts are those of Germanic-derived phrasal verbs into nouns. These new forms are felt to be more forceful and vigorous than those Latin-derived synonyms which they so often supplant. Although considerable latitude is shown at present in the use of hyphens, I have here printed them all solid.

breakaway	secession
breakdown	(a) collapse, failure of health or power
	(b) analysis
breakout	violent escape
breakthrough	sudden advance, surmounting of barriers to progress
breakup	disintegration, disruption, dispersal
buildup	gradual increase
dropout	reject
followup	sequel
frameup	conspiracy
getaway	escape
getby	method of survival
getout	withdrawal from an embarrassing situation
gettogether	informal social gathering
getup	costume, outfit
hideout	place of refuge
holdup	obstruction
hookup	(a) linking of related parts (electronics, mechanics)
	(b) radio or television network
layout	arrangement, plan
leadin	introduction
leftover	remainder, remnant
letup	relaxation, relief
makeup	(a) application of cosmetics
	(b) composition, constitution
payoff	recompense, compensation
rakeoff	reception of illicit profits
sellout	betrayal
setback	reverse, defeat

setup	organization
shakeup	drastic overhaul
shareout	distribution
showdown	final disclosure
stepup	escalation
takeoff	(a) becoming airborne (aviation)
	(b) humorous mimicry
takeover	assumption of control
throwaway	free advertisement folder or broadside
walkout	(a) strike by workers
	(b) ostentatious departure from a meeting as an expression of protest
walkover	effortless triumph

Among other recent creations are those *-in* forms, still hyphened, especially *teach-in* (1962) and *pray-in* (1968) which are modelled on the *stay-in* or *sit-in* strikes of the nineteenth century. In such industrial disputes, also called *sit-down* strikes, the workers occupied the factory floor and refused to budge. In a *lock-out* strike the employers closed the factory gates against the workers.[1] A *teach-in* is a prolonged series of lectures and seminars held in defiance of university authorities. It was first used as a protest against the establishment of the United States military council in South Vietnam on 8 February 1962. *Pray-in* was first employed in August 1968 when lay congregations occupied cathedrals and churches in protest against Pope Paul VI's encyclical *Humanae vitae* banning birth control.

---

[1] *Strike*, short for *strike of* (= from) *work*, was first used as a term in collective bargaining in 1810. It has since been adopted into other European languages (G *Streik*, Dutch *strijk*, Swedish *strejk*). As shown by a report in *The Annual Register* for the year 1768, section 92, its source in this sense arose in the Royal Navy: 'A body of sailors.. . . proceeded . . . to Sunderland and at the cross there read a paper, setting forth their grievances . . . After this they went on board the several ships in that harbour, and *struck* (lowered down) their yards, in order to prevent them from proceeding to sea'. See OED s.v. *strike*, v. 17.

OTHER RECENT CONVERSIONS

When I first heard the refrain of a 1965 pop song –

> *Though I search the whole world through*
> *I'll never find another you*

– I was much struck by the pleasing audacity of what I took to be a novel type of conversion. On second thoughts, however, it slowly dawned upon me that such a pronoun-into-noun conversion was as old as Shakespeare. Yes, centuries ago (in *Twelfth Night* I v 26) Viola spoke for all mankind when she so gently and so eloquently reproved the fair Countess Olivia for declining love:

> *Lady, you are the cruellest* she *alive*
> *If you will lead these graces to the grave*
> *And leave the world no copy.*

Only a few years later Richard Crashaw (in the opening verses of *Wishes. To his supposed Mistresse*) envisaged his all-too-fanciful lady love:

> *Who'er she be –*
> *That not impossible* She
> *That shall command my heart and me.*

Today beguiling beauticians assure us flatteringly that 'a lovelier *you* will leave our beauty parlour'.

Among other recent conversions we observe the following:

Our cook likes to *brown* the potatoes (adjective into verb)
The admiral *upped* (promoted) the young seaman on the spot (adverb into verb)
My uncle *pooh-poohed* the whole plan (interjection into verb)
Is Mary's new baby a *he*? (pronoun into noun)
The manager has a fit of the *blues* (adjective into noun)
You should know all the *ins* and *outs* by now (adverbs into nouns)
Are you a *has-been* or a *might-have-been*? (verbal group into noun)

Better to be an *also-ran* than a *never-was* (adverb + verb into noun)

Would you like a *with* or a *without* (referring to cups of tea with or without sugar)? (prepositions into nouns)

If *ifs* and *ans* were pots and pans, there would be no trade for tinkers (conjunctions into nouns)[1]

Here you have the *master* key (noun into adjective)

John's father was a *he*-man (pronoun into adjective)[2]

Harold Macmillan was the *then* Prime Minister (adverb into adjective)

LIMITS OF FUNCTIONAL SHIFT

An unusual grammatical conversion need not necessarily hamper comprehension. A child will understand at once if it is told that 'this water is scalding hot' or 'freezing cold' – hot to the extent of scalding, or cold to the extent of freezing (gerund into intensive adverb). Since about 1955, the direct assertion 'For you this is a *must*' has acquired a widespread vogue through television advertising. The reason is not far to seek. With its personal appeal, its six-syllable brevity, its pleasing rhythm, and its emphatic cadence, it has the highest verbal value. It is far more potent and cogent than, say, 'For you this is an utter necessity' or 'You cannot possibly get along without this'. At the moment, however, it is the only modal auxiliary that can be thus daringly shifted. No advertiser would now risk saying 'For you this is a *could*' meaning 'You, yes you, could bring this off if you really put your back into it'; or 'For you this is a *should*' meaning 'You, yes you, should and ought to do this if you fully woke up to your moral responsibilities'.

Are there, then, any limits set to functional shifts in present-day English? Yes, you will surely have observed that the shifts described in this chapter have all been made in the direction of full words: verbs and nouns mostly, adjectives and

[1] Nineteenth century proverb. Logically the forms *ifs* and *ans* are 'named', not 'used'.

[2] Morphologically *he*- is not a free form, but a component of a compound word.

adverbs rarely. Otherwise there are no limits. The tagmemic slots of inherited patterns can be filled freely and variously according to style and purpose. That possibility holds only because sentence frames are well established and because word order remains adequately stable throughout the whole English-speaking world.

SELECT BIBLIOGRAPHY

CHAPTER 1

In *An Introduction to the Pronunciation of English*, London, Arnold 1962, A. C. Gimson describes expertly many of the sound changes actually going on in present-day speech. He is now engaged on a revision of the late Daniel Jones's *English Pronouncing Dictionary*, London, Dent, twelfth edition 1963, which will long remain the leading authority on the pronunciation of British English. For United States English the most recent book is Charles Kenneth Thomas, *An Introduction to the Phonetics of American English*, New York, Ronald Press, second edition 1958. For Australian English we are fortunate in having G. W. Turner, *The English Language in Australia and New Zealand*, London, Longmans 1966. The third and longest chapter in Charles Barber's *Linguistic Change in Present-Day English*, Edinburgh, Oliver and Boyd 1964, is concerned entirely with changes in pronunciation.

CHAPTER 2

The most recent study of the relationship between sounds and symbols is that by Axel Wijk, *Rules of Pronunciation for the English Language: An Account of the Relationship between English Spelling and Pronunciation*, OUP 1966. It inevitably covers the same ground as those two authentic studies by Sir William Alexander Craigie, *English Spelling: Its Rules and Reasons*, OUP 1927, and *Some Anomalies of Spelling*, SPE Tract 59, 1942.

The two professional manuals for the Style of the House (often abbreviated as APD and RCR) are Frederick Howard Collins, *The Authors' and Printers' Dictionary, a guide for Authors, Editors, Printers, Correctors of the Press, Compositors, and Typists*; and Horace Hart, *Rules for Compositors and Readers at the University Press, Oxford*, 37th edition, completely revised and reset, OUP 1967.

The best general account of the whole subject viewed on its

historical background is George Henry Vallin's *Spelling*, competently revised by Donald George Scragg, London, Deutsch 1965. This detailed study is sensible, exact, and informative. It also contains a supplementary chapter on American orthography by John Williams Clark of the University of Minnesota.

Anyone interested in controversial issues will find abundant food for thought in Mont Follick's *The Case for Spelling Reform*, London, Pitman 1965.

CHAPTER 3

Mary Sydney Serjeantson's *A History of Foreign Words in English*, London, Kegan Paul 1935, remains the most comprehensive work on loan words. It has been admirably supplemented by Alan Bliss in *A Dictionary of Foreign Words and Phrases in Current English*, London, Routledge 1966, which contains in an Appendix extensive lists of recent borrowings from both European and non-European sources.

Three guides to current usage, two British and one American, contain most valuable critical comments on new words: Fowler-Gowers, *A Dictionary of Modern English Usage*, OUP 1965; Eric Partridge, *Usage and Abusage, A Guide to Good English*, London, Hamish Hamilton, sixth edition 1965; and Bergen and Cornelia Evans, *A Dictionary of Contemporary American Usage*, New York, Random House 1957.

Neologisms are discussed in Chapter 4, *The Growth of the Vocabulary*, in Charles Barber's *Linguistic Change in Present-Day English*, already mentioned. John Moore's *You English Words*, London, Collins 1961, consists of a series of delightful essays on various aspects of our vocabulary, the last of which, entitled *The Ever-changing Language*, is by far the longest. In *The Changing English Language*, London, Macmillan 1968, Brian Foster is mainly concerned with American influences on British English.

Ernest Weekley's numerous books are highly entertaining, from *The Romance of Words* (1912) to *Words and Names* (1933). So, too, are Ivor Brown's erudite discourses, from *A*

Word in Your Ear (1942) to *Words in Season* (1961). Different, but no less illuminating, are Stuart Chase's *The Tyranny of Words* (1938) and *Power of Words* (1955).

CHAPTER 4

Theodore H. Savory's *The Language of Science*, London, Deutsch, revised edition 1967, stands unrivalled as a brief, lucid and reliable account of the origin and growth of scientific English. *The Greek Legacy* is the title of Chapter 7 in *The Mother Tongue*, London, Secker and Warburg 1964, by Lancelot Hogben, that versatile author of *Mathematics for the Million* and *Science for the Citizen*.

Fifty-one 'lessons' for undergraduates are provided by Donald M. Ayers in *English Words from Latin and Greek Elements*, Tucson, Arizona UP 1965. Still more recently, a large and attractive handbook to the International Code of Botanical Nomenclature called *Botanical Latin*, London, Nelson 1967, has been compiled by William T. Stearn of the Natural History Department at the British Museum.

Advanced expositions of nominal groups are given by Robert B. Lees in *The Grammar of English Nominalizations*, Bloomington, Indiana UP 1960, and by Yakov Malkiel in *Studies in Irreversible Binomials*, comprising Chapter 12 of *Essays on Linguistic Themes*, Oxford, Blackwell 1968. Among the many grammar books devoting some attention to changing nominal groups, the following may be consulted: Charles Carpenter Fries, *The Structure of English*, New York, Harcourt, Brace and Company 1952, pp. 142–201; James Sledd, *A Short Introduction to English Grammar*, Chicago, Scott, Foresman and Company 1959, pp. 114–120; Winthrop Nelson Francis, *The Structure of American English*, New York, Ronald Press 1954, pp. 237–252; and Ralph Bernard Long, *The Sentence and Its Parts, A Grammar of Contemporary English*, Chicago UP 1961, pp. 228–356.

CHAPTER 6

Descriptions of anomalous finites are given in the preliminary notes to *The Advanced Learner's Dictionary of Current English*, edited by A. S. Hornby, E. V. Gatenby and H. Wakefield, OUP, second edition 1963, pp. ix–xiv; A. S. Hornby, *A Guide to Patterns and Usage in English*, OUP 1962, pp. 1–15; Martin Joos, *The English Verb, Form and Meanings*, Wisconsin UP 1964, pp. 53–73; and F. R. Palmer, *A Linguistic Study of the English Verb*, London, Longmans 1965, pp. 19–42.

CHAPTER 7

Paul Christophersen's Copenhagen dissertation on *The Articles, A Study of their Theory and Use in English*, OUP 1939, offers a good beginning to the study of determiners on their historical background. Two other Scandinavian doctoral theses throw new light on the contemporary scene: Sverker Brorström, *The Increasing Frequency of the Preposition ABOUT during the Modern English Period* (Stockholm Studies in English IX) Stockholm, Almqvist and Wiksell 1963; and Sven Jacobson, *Adverbial Positions in English*, Stockholm, Tofters Tryckeri 1964. Lively discussions on changing pronouns, and many other features touched on in this chapter, will be found in Randolph Quirk's *The Use of English*, London, Longmans, second edition revised 1968. My model for attributive adjectives should be closely compared with the table on p. 41 of Winthrop Nelson Francis's *The English Language, An Introduction*, New York, Norton 1967.

CHAPTER 8

My schema for simple sentence frames should be closely compared with *Sentence Situations* II and III in Harold Whitehall's *Structural Essentials of English*, London, Longmans 1951, pp. 38–39. Although written so long ago, Henry Sweet's *A New English Grammar Logical and Historical*, OUP Part I 1891, Part II 1898, is astonishingly forward looking, anticipating the doctrines of subsequent structural, functional and transformational grammarians. Functional shifts have since been well described by R. W. Zandvoort in *A Handbook of English Grammar*, London, Longmans, fourth edition 1966. The relations between form, function and content have been well formulated by Knud Schibsbye in *A Modern English Grammar*, OUP 1965.

Subject Index

Word Index